Why Won't you listen?

THE SCIENCE OF **WHAT KIDS REALLY HEAR** WHEN YOU SPEAK

(THEY'RE NOT DEFYING YOU)

DAVID A. SMITH

A Guide for Parents, Teachers, and
Anyone Who Talks to Kids

To my daughters,

Who showed me that the most important conversations happen in the space between what we say and what is heard.

This book exists because of what we discovered together.

Recognition Press
P.O. Box 3
Nashotah Wisconsin
www.recognitionpress.com

ISBN: 979-8-9997309-0-9 (paperback)
       979-8-9997309-1-6 (ebook)

First Edition: 2025
Printed in the United States of America

Important Notice:

This book offers one framework for understanding why children seem not to listen. The "universe" metaphor helps explain real developmental phenomena in practical terms. When I describe children asking "let's say 300 questions a day," I'm helping you grasp the relentless nature of their curiosity, not citing research.

The core insights—that children process language differently than adults, that abstract concepts develop slowly, that context dramatically affects behavior—reflect established developmental principles. My interpretation through "universe-building" is one way to make sense of your daily experience.

The observations in this book:

- Are based on general patterns observed in research, primarily from English-speaking Western contexts

- Represent typical developmental trends with significant individual variation

- Use approximate age ranges and processing speeds that vary widely among children

- May not apply to bilingual, multilingual, or non-Western language development

- Should not be used to diagnose or label any child

The strategies and insights presented are meant to help readers understand common language development patterns. Every child is unique and develops at their own pace. Some children may require specialized support. If you have concerns about your child's development, language acquisition, or behavior, please consult with your pediatrician or a qualified developmental specialist.

While this book addresses typical language development, neurodivergent children—including those with autism spectrum conditions, ADHD, language processing differences, or other developmental variations—may process language differently. These differences are not deficits but variations that may benefit from different approaches. Parents of neurodivergent children are encouraged to work with specialists familiar with their child's specific needs.

A Note on Examples, Numbers, and Patterns:

All examples in this book illustrate patterns documented in child development research and represent behaviors commonly observed across many children. The specific scenarios and children described are composites created for illustrative purposes. Any resemblance to specific individuals is coincidental.

This book uses varied pronouns (he, she, they) throughout examples to reflect the diversity of children and families.

Bulk Sales: For information about special discounts for bulk purchases for educational use, premiums, or fundraising, please contact Recognition Press.

Translation Rights: For information about translation rights, please contact Recognition Press.

Audio Rights: Recognition Press Audio edition published by Recognition Press Narrated by [to be confirmed]

Cover design by: Ikhen Kenny
Interior design by: Command-S

CONTENTS

Part V: Different Contexts, Different Children

Part VI: Building Bridges

Part VII: Your Toolkit

Practical Appendix

The Cookie Incident

Here's something that happened yesterday. Or last week. Or five minutes ago in millions of homes.

A four-year-old takes a cookie.
Mom says, *"I'm disappointed."* The child keeps eating.
Mom's frustration rises.
"Did you hear me? I said I'm disappointed!"
The child looks up, confused. Still chewing.
Mom sees defiance. The child sees... what exactly?

When Mom says "disappointed," she's transmitting an entire universe of meaning: expectations not met, feeling let down but not angry, still loving you, wishing you'd made a different choice. Perhaps there's even a memory of her own mother's disappointed face, the weight of that particular word in her family's emotional vocabulary.

The four-year-old hears: *Mom said a word. She looks unhappy.*

That's it. That's all.

Not because the child doesn't care. But because "disappointed" isn't just a word—it's an entire constellation of experiences, emotions, and abstract concepts that take years to build. The child literally doesn't have the neural architecture yet to receive the full transmission.

It's like Mom is broadcasting in 5G while the child is receiving on a flip phone from 2003.

And here's what's fascinating—and maybe a bit relieving: We do this all day. Every day. Then we wonder why kids don't listen.

The Universal Scene

Perhaps you've lived this scene: You're at Target. Your three-year-old is melting down because you won't buy the toy they just discovered existed four seconds ago. You hear yourself saying words your parents said: "You're being ridiculous." "People are watching." "I'm losing my patience."

But what if your child literally doesn't understand what "patience" is? What if "ridiculous" is just a sound that means "Mom's face is red"? What if the concept of strangers judging behavior is as foreign to them as quantum physics?

You're not failing. You're speaking different languages while using the same words.

Try This: The Translation Check

Here's something that might surprise you. Find your child when they're calm and fed—maybe during that golden hour after snack but before dinner chaos. Casually ask:

> *"What does 'pay attention' mean?"*
>
> Your child will probably say: *"Look at you"* or *"Watch you."*
>
> What you think it means: *"Listen carefully, think about my words, process the information, and remember what I'm saying for future use."*

See the canyon between those definitions? When you say "pay attention," your child obediently looks at you. Mission accomplished (in their mind). Meanwhile, you're frustrated they're not absorbing your carefully crafted explanation about why we don't paint the cat.

They're not defying you. They literally think "pay attention" means "point your eyes at someone."

The Gap Nobody Mentioned

What if I told you that the space between what you say and what your child hears is so vast, it's a miracle any communication happens at all? And what if understanding this gap—really understanding it—could transform every interaction you have with your child?

That gap between what you say and what they hear? That's what this book is about.

But perhaps more importantly, it's about releasing the guilt you carry when communication fails. It's about understanding that your frustration is valid AND your child's confusion is valid. Both can be true. Both ARE true.

A Different Kind of Parenting Book

Maybe you've read parenting books that made you feel like you're doing everything wrong. Books that suggest if you just followed these 47 steps perfectly, your child would transform into a compliant, emotionally regulated tiny adult.

This isn't that book.

This book won't tell you how to make your child listen better. Instead, it might help you understand what they're actually hearing. And perhaps, just maybe, that understanding will change everything—not because you'll become a perfect parent (that doesn't exist), but because you'll finally see what's really happening in those moments of miscommunication.

You'll discover why your child can remember every *Pokemon* evolution but can't remember to flush the toilet. Why they can follow complex video game rules but can't follow "be good at grandma's." Why they're angels at school and tornados at home.

It's not manipulation. It's not defiance. It's something much more interesting—and once you see it, you can't unsee it.

PART I

The Discovery

CHAPTER 1

The Invisible Gap

Has anyone ever taught you how children actually understand words? Probably Not.

Sure, you learned they develop language in stages. First words around twelve months. Two-word combinations by age two. Sentences by three. But nobody mentioned the enormous gap between saying words and understanding their full meaning.

It's not a conspiracy. It's just that until recently, we didn't really know. The research is barely a generation old. Your parents didn't know because the science didn't exist yet. Your teachers didn't know because it wasn't in their training. Your pediatrician might know the milestones but probably not the mechanics.

So here you are, doing what every generation before you has done: assuming that when children say words, they understand them the way you do. It's such a logical assumption that questioning it feels absurd.

The Museum Moment

Let me share something that might sound familiar.

> A mother takes her five-year-old to a museum.
> *"Be respectful of the artwork,"* she says.
>
> The child nods solemnly. Three minutes later,
> he's touching everything.
>
> *"I TOLD you to be respectful!"* she hisses.
>
> *"I am!"* he insists, genuinely confused.

Here's what happened: To the mother, "respectful of artwork" means:

- Don't touch
- Speak quietly
- Move slowly
- Stand at appropriate distance
- Appreciate without interfering
- Understand the artwork's value to others
- Recognize the museum as a shared space

To the child, "respectful" meant... actually, he had no idea. Maybe it meant "walk nicely"? He was walking nicely. Mission accomplished.

The mother thinks she's been clear. The child thinks he's complying. They're both right. They're both wrong. They're operating in different universes.

The Generational Echo

Think about your own childhood for a moment. Remember being told to "behave"? Did anyone ever actually explain what that meant? Or did you gradually, through trial and error and lots of getting in trouble, piece together that "behave" meant different things in different situations?

"Behave" at church meant: sit still, be quiet, don't kick the pew. "Behave" at grandma's meant: don't break anything, eat what's served, hug even if you don't want to. "Behave" at the store meant: don't ask for things, stay close, don't touch.

You learned through confusion, through mistakes, through that hot shame of getting it wrong in public. And now, perhaps without meaning to, you're expecting your child to just know what you mean. Because that's how it's always been done.

The Daily Misfire

It happens dozens of times a day, these small miscommunications that build into frustration:

MORNING: *"Get ready for school."*

You mean: Get dressed, brush teeth, pack backpack, eat breakfast, find shoes, remember library book.

They hear: Put on one sock.

AFTERNOON: *"Clean up your mess."*

You mean: Return items to proper locations, throw away trash, wipe surfaces.

They hear: Push things into a pile.

EVENING: *"Settle down."*

You mean: Lower your voice, slow your body, prepare for sleep transition.

They hear: ???

(Seriously, what does "settle" mean to a four-year-old?)

Each misfire adds to the frustration pile. By bedtime, you're both exhausted from trying to communicate across this invisible gap.

What If It's Not Defiance?

Here's a thought that might reshape how you see your child: What if most of what looks like defiance is actually confusion?

What if your child isn't ignoring you but literally doesn't understand what you're asking?

What if they're not being difficult but are genuinely trying to navigate a world where the rules seem to change constantly and nobody explains why?

Consider this: Your child successfully follows incredibly complex rules all day long. They know that:

- You can run on grass but not in hallways
- You can yell outside but not in the library
- You can jump on trampolines but not beds (usually)
- You can throw balls but not toys
- You can splash in the bath but not in puddles (unless wearing boots?)

That's an incredibly complex set of contextual rules they're managing. Maybe they're not bad at listening. Maybe we're not great at explaining.

The Translator's Burden

Without realizing it, you've become a translator between two universes—the adult world of abstract concepts and unspoken rules, and your child's world of concrete, immediate experience. But here's the thing: nobody trained you for this job. Nobody gave you the dictionary.

You're winging it, just like your parents did, just like their parents did. The difference is, now we have windows into what's actually happening in children's brains when language develops. We can see the gap. We can map it. We can build bridges across it.

But first, we have to recognize it exists.

The Exhaustion Explained

Perhaps you've wondered why parenting is so exhausting. Sure, there's the physical stuff—the constant motion, the vigilance, the sleep deprivation. But there's something else, isn't there? A mental exhaustion that's harder to explain.

What if I told you that you're doing simultaneous translation all day long without realizing it? Every instruction, every explanation, every correction requires you to:

1. Formulate the thought in adult language
2. Somehow sense it won't compute
3. Attempt to translate on the fly
4. Realize the translation failed
5. Try again with growing frustration
6. Eventually just physically intervene

No wonder you're tired. You're running translation software in the background of every interaction, and it's draining your battery.

The Pattern Recognition

Maybe you've noticed patterns but couldn't quite name them:

- Your child listens better when they're well-rested (their translation software works better)
- Instructions work better with gestures (visual translation support)
- They follow rules better at school (clearer, more consistent universe)
- They struggle more when hungry (translation software offline)
- They understand grandma better than grandpa (different translation styles)

These aren't random. They're clues to how the translation process works and breaks down.

A Different Lens

This gap in our collective understanding has created a peculiar situation. We're all walking around with expert-level expectations for beginner-level brains. It's like expecting someone to read a map of a city they've never visited, in a language they're still learning, while also learning what a map even is.

The frustration you feel when a child doesn't follow "simple" instructions? That's the gap revealing itself. The confusion when they follow rules perfectly at school but not at home? That's the gap too. The bafflement when they melt down over seemingly nothing? Gap again.

The Permission to Struggle

Here's something nobody says enough: It's okay that this is hard. It's okay that you lose your patience. It's okay that sometimes you have no idea what your child is thinking or why they did what they did.

You're not failing. You're operating without crucial information that simply wasn't available until very recently. Information that changes everything once you have it.

This isn't about becoming a different kind of parent or teacher. It's about seeing what's actually happening. Like finally getting glasses after years of squinting—you weren't doing anything wrong before. You just couldn't see clearly.

The Shift

The beautiful thing? Once you understand the gap, you can't unsee it. And that natural awareness, without any extra effort, starts to change how you interact with children. Not because you're trying harder, but because you finally understand what you're actually asking of them.

You might find yourself naturally:

- Slowing down your speech
- Using more concrete language
- Adding gestures without thinking
- Being more patient with confusion
- Recognizing exhaustion's effect on understanding

Not because you're following some expert's rules, but because you can see what's happening.

What's Coming

In the chapters ahead, we'll explore this gap from every angle. You'll discover:

- Why your child can't process the word "don't" (Chapter 12)
- What's really happening during the midnight water cup crisis (Chapter 10)

But perhaps more importantly, you'll gain a new lens for seeing your child's behavior. Instead of "Why won't they listen?" you might find yourself wondering "What are they actually hearing?"

And that shift—from frustration to curiosity—changes everything.

The Bridge Builder

You're about to become conscious of something you've been doing unconsciously all along: building bridges across the communication gap. But now, with awareness, you can build better bridges. Stronger ones. Clearer ones.

This isn't about perfection. It's about understanding. And understanding, it turns out, is enough.

No guilt required. No generational healing necessary. Just clarity about what's really going on when we talk to children.

Welcome to the gap. Let's explore it together.

CHAPTER 2

The Iceberg Problem

Watch a two-year-old at the zoo. They point at the elephant and say "big doggy!" The parent corrects them: "No sweetie, that's an elephant." The child nods sagely. "Ephant." Problem solved, right?

Not quite.

The child has learned a sound. A label. Like putting a sticky note on a filing cabinet they can't open yet. Inside that cabinet should eventually be:

- How elephants differ from dogs (beyond size)
- That elephants live in different places
- The concept of wild versus domestic
- That pointing at large people and saying "elephant" is socially problematic (learned this one the hard way at Walmart)
- Memory capabilities that put your smartphone to shame
- Complex social structures
- The whole trunk situation

But right now? It's just a sound that makes adults happy when you say it near the big gray thing.

The Naming Illusion

We adults have this adorable belief that once a child can name something, they understand it. It's like thinking that because someone can say "bonjour," they speak French.

My neighbor's three-year-old can flawlessly identify and name:

- Every construction vehicle known to mankind
- All the dinosaurs (including ones I'm pretty sure paleontologists made up)
- Every character from Paw Patrol including their specific skills

Ask him what "tomorrow" means? Blank stare. Ask him to "be patient"? Might as well be speaking Klingon.

He's not behind. He's just showing us that naming and understanding are completely different universes. Knowing the word "excavator" doesn't mean he understands "disappointed."

The Kitchen Incident

Here's a scene that plays out in kitchens worldwide:

"Honey, please set the table nicely for dinner."

The six-year-old springs into action. Five minutes later, you find:

- Forks randomly distributed
- Napkins in a pile in the center
- Cups at the wrong seats
- Spoons inexplicably in the living room
- One plate on the floor (for the dog, obviously)

"I said set it NICELY!"
"I did!"

And here's the thing—in their universe, they absolutely did. "Nicely" to them meant... energetically? Without breaking anything? With good intentions?

To you, *"nicely"* contained:

- Proper placement protocol
- Aesthetic considerations
- Social conventions about place settings
- Understanding of meal progression
- Respect for shared dining
- Cultural expectations you absorbed over decades

That's not an instruction. That's an entire semester of finishing school compressed into one word.

Every Word Is An Iceberg

Perhaps you've seen those iceberg diagrams where 90% is underwater? That's every word you say to your child. They see the tip. You see the whole mountain of ice beneath the surface. Then we get frustrated when they crash into it.

Let's take a seemingly simple word: **"Share."**

THE TIP (what your child sees):

- Give toy to other person
- They stop crying maybe

THE UNDERWATER MOUNTAIN (what you see):

- Social reciprocity expectations
- Building relationships through generosity
- Delayed gratification for future benefit
- Fairness concepts
- Turn-taking protocols
- Community building

- Conflict resolution
- Emotional regulation while giving up something you want
- Trust that items will return
- Understanding that sharing creates positive feelings in others
- The whole "sharing is caring" philosophical framework

When your three-year-old "shares" by throwing a toy at another child's head, they're not being aggressive. They're attempting to execute "give toy to other person" with the sophistication of someone using a chainsaw to perform surgery.

The Instructions That Aren't

Think about giving a five-year-old what seems like simple instructions: "Put your toys away before dinner."

YOU MEAN:

- Gather all items that belong to you
- Determine their designated storage locations
- Place them there in an organized fashion
- Complete this within the next 20 minutes
- Because we eat at 6 PM
- This is a daily expectation
- It shows responsibility and respect for shared spaces
- Also please don't shove everything under your bed and call it done

THEY HEAR:

- Toys (which ones? The ones I'm playing with? All toys that exist?)
- Away (where's that? Away from what? How far is away?)
- Dinner (that thing that happens eventually)

The child standing there looking confused isn't being difficult. They're trying to decode your transmission with about 10% of the necessary equipment.

The Bathroom Directive Disaster

"Go get ready for bed"

Such a simple request. Let's unpack what this actually means:

YOUR UNIVERSE of "get ready for bed":

1. Go to bathroom
2. Use toilet (completely empty bladder for night)
3. Wash hands (with soap, for 20 seconds)
4. Brush teeth (all surfaces, 2 minutes)
5. Floss (haha, just kidding, nobody flosses)
6. Wash face
7. Change into pajamas (weather-appropriate)
8. Put dirty clothes in hamper
9. Select tomorrow's outfit (optional but appreciated)
10. Get into bed with selected stuffed animals
11. Mentally prepare for sleep

YOUR CHILD'S UNIVERSE of "get ready for bed":

1. Exist near bedroom
2. Maybe remove one shoe
3. Complain about not being tired
4. Remember urgent need for water/snack/bathroom

Twenty minutes later you find them naked except for one sock, playing with toothpaste, having flooded the bathroom sink. They're not defying you. They got lost somewhere between your universe and theirs.

The Apology Archaeology

*Let's dig deeper into "sorry"—perhaps the most
misunderstood word in the parent-child dictionary.*

LAYER 1 (Around age 2): Sorry is a magic sound that stops adult anger

LAYER 2 (Around age 3): Sorry is required after hitting

LAYER 3 (Around age 4): Sorry involves looking sad (performance improves)

LAYER 4 (Around age 5): Sorry means something bad happened

LAYER 5 (Around age 6): Sorry might mean I did the bad thing

LAYER 6 (Around age 7): Sorry means I shouldn't have done that

LAYER 7 (Around age 8): Sorry means I feel bad that you feel bad

LAYER 8 (Around age 9+): Sorry encompasses remorse, responsibility, and repair

When your three-year-old says "SORRY!" while actively
continuing the offensive behavior, they're not being sarcastic.
They're at Layer 1, successfully executing the magic sound while
you're expecting Layer 8.

The "Clean Your Room" Comedy

Perhaps the most universe-collision-prone instruction in
parenting: "Clean your room."

PARENT'S "CLEAN" UNIVERSE:

- Floor visible
- Items in designated locations
- Bed made
- Surfaces clear
- Clothes in dresser/closet
- Trash in trash can

- Could photograph for real estate listing
- Marie Kondo would approve

CHILD'S "CLEAN" UNIVERSE (Around age 4):

- Can walk without stepping on Legos (mostly)
- Favorite toy visible
- That smell is gone

CHILD'S "CLEAN" UNIVERSE (Around age 7):

- Created a path
- Shoved things in closet
- Covered mess with blanket
- Sprayed Febreze (learned from teenager sibling)

CHILD'S "CLEAN" UNIVERSE (Around age 10):

- Organized chaos
- "I know where everything is"
- Clean enough that parents won't check closely
- Strategic placement of a few visible clean spots

The evolution of "clean" understanding is a years-long construction project. Yet we expect immediate comprehension. It's like asking someone to perform Shakespeare on their first day of English class.

The Feelings Iceberg

Perhaps nowhere is the iceberg problem more evident than with emotion words. "I'm frustrated with you."

WHAT YOU'RE COMMUNICATING:

- I had expectations
- You didn't meet them
- I'm managing my anger
- This is disappointment mixed with irritation

- I still love you
- But I need space
- And you need to reflect on your choices
- This feeling will pass
- But behavior change is needed

WHAT YOUR FOUR-YEAR-OLD HEARS:

- Mom has angry face
- Something about me
- Frustrated is a word
- Still don't know what I did
- Maybe if I hug her?

They're not being emotionally obtuse. They're trying to understand an emotion word that requires experiences they haven't had yet. It's like trying to explain "nostalgia" to someone who has no past to be nostalgic about.

The Context Iceberg

Here's something fun: Words change their icebergs depending on context.

"Quiet" at library = whisper, tiptoe, exist gently
"Quiet" at home = stop screaming, probably
"Quiet" at movie = can whisper to parent
"Quiet" at bedtime = no talking but singing okay?
"Quiet" at restaurant = inside voice but not whisper
"Quiet" during baby's nap = become a ninja

Your child isn't being deliberately obtuse when they use their "library quiet" at home (essentially becoming mute) or their "home quiet" at library (still yelling, just slightly less). They're trying to match the word to the context with incomplete universe maps.

The Possession Problem

"That's mine!"

Simple concept, right? Ownership. Possession. Basic property rights. Except "mine" contains multitudes:

- Legal ownership
- Temporary possession
- Emotional attachment
- Fair distribution
- Property rights
- Sharing exceptions
- Family versus personal property
- Borrowing protocols
- The difference between "turn" and "ownership"

When a three-year-old claims the grocery store is "mine" because they're in it, they're not being ridiculous. They're working with a simplified definition: "Mine = thing I'm currently experiencing."

Building Above the Waterline

So what do we do with all these icebergs floating around?

Perhaps we start by recognizing that every word we say carries decades of underwater meaning that children find it difficult to see yet. Maybe we get curious about what they actually understand rather than frustrated about what they don't.

Try This: The Iceberg Check

Pick a word you use often. Let's say "careful." Now draw an actual iceberg:

ABOVE WATER (what your child might understand):
- Move slowly
- Mom looks worried

BELOW WATER (what you mean):
- Assess environment for dangers
- Predict consequences
- Modify behavior accordingly
- Consider impact on objects/others
- Maintain awareness
- Exercise impulse control
- Remember previous careful-requiring situations
- Apply lessons learned
- Value preservation over experimentation

Suddenly their failure to be "careful" makes more sense. They're operating with 5% of the concept while you're expecting 100% execution.

The beauty is, once you see the iceberg, you can help them build it piece by piece instead of expecting them to magically understand the whole thing.

CHAPTER 3

The Universe Inside "Sorry"

Let's watch a three-year-old hit their sister.

> Parent intervenes: *"Say sorry."*
> *"SORRY!"* the child shouts, then immediately hits again.
> Parent, exasperated: *"I said apologize!"*
> *"I DID!"*

Who's right here? Plot twist: Both of them. And that's the problem.

The Magic Word Academy

Somewhere around age two, children enter what I call the Magic Word Academy. They learn that certain sounds have power:

- *"Please"* = adults give you things
- *"Thank you"* = adults smile

- **"Sorry"** = angry face becomes normal face
- **"Excuse me"** = people move
- **"Help"** = adults do things for you

These aren't words with meaning. They're spells. They're cheat codes. They're buttons that produce predictable responses.

Your toddler has learned that "sorry" is the sound that fixes adult anger. They've mastered the mechanics perfectly. When adult face looks like *this*, make the "sorry" sound. Problem solved. System reset. Ready to play again.

The Sorry Spectrum

For the child, "sorry" is a magic word that makes angry adults stop being angry. It's a sound that fixes things. Like pressing CTRL+Z on the universe.

For the adult, **"sorry"** carries an entire universe:

- Recognition of wrongdoing
- Empathy for the injured party
- Genuine remorse
- Intention to change behavior
- Understanding of social contracts
- The complex dance of rupture and repair in relationships
- Acknowledgment of harm caused
- Acceptance of responsibility
- Commitment to making amends
- Understanding that trust was damaged

The child said the word. They did exactly what was asked. They just didn't transmit any of the universe that's supposed to come with it. Because that universe doesn't exist in their brain yet.

It's like asking someone to send an email before they understand electricity exists.

The Restaurant Apology Disaster

Scene: Nice restaurant. Your four-year-old accidentally-on-purpose spills their juice.

> You: *"Say sorry to the waiter."*
> Child (cheerfully): *"Sorry waiter!"*
> Waiter: *"It's okay, accidents happen."*
> Child: (immediately knocks over water glass)
> You: *"I said SORRY!"*
> Child: *"I SAID IT!"*

The child isn't being defiant. In their universe, they executed the protocol perfectly:

1. Adult requested the sorry sound
2. Sorry sound was produced
3. Waiter said okay
4. System reset
5. Ready for next action

The fact that "sorry" should prevent repetition of the behavior? That connection doesn't exist yet. It's like being frustrated that pressing "save" on a document doesn't also edit the content.

The Sibling Sorry Situation

Perhaps nowhere is the sorry gap more evident than with siblings:

> 5-year-old takes 3-year-old's toy
> Parent: *"Give it back and say sorry."*

5-year-old: *"Sorry"* (while death-gripping the toy)

Parent: *"You have to mean it."*

5-year-old: (blank stare) *"Soooorrrryyyy?"* (trying different intonation)

Parent: *"And give the toy back!"*

5-year-old: *"But I said sorry!"*

In their universe, sorry is the price you pay to keep the toy. Like putting a quarter in a parking meter. They paid the sorry tax. Transaction complete. Why are you still talking about the toy?

What's Actually Happening in That Three-Year-Old Brain

Here's the neural play-by-play when a three-year-old hits their sister and you demand an apology:

0 seconds: Want toy sister has

1 second: Hit sister (successful toy acquisition!)

2 seconds: Mom face changed (uh oh)

3 seconds: Mom says words (something about sorry)

4 seconds: Say "sorry" (the fixing sound)

5 seconds: Mom still has angry face (confusing)

6 seconds: Say "sorry" louder (maybe volume is issue?)

7 seconds: Mom taking toy away (system failure)

8 seconds: Complete meltdown (universe collapse)

At no point did the concept of "I hurt someone and feel bad about it" enter the equation. Not because your child is a sociopath, but because that neural pathway doesn't exist yet.

The Developmental Timeline of Sorry

Around age 2: The Sound

- Sorry is a noise adults require
- Like "bye-bye" or "night-night"
- Pure performance, zero comprehension

Around age 3: The Transaction

- Sorry is payment for infractions
- Say it, debt cleared
- Still no emotional content

Around age 4: The Consequence

- Sorry happens after bad things
- Starting to connect action to response
- But still mostly performative

Around age 5: The Feeling Emerges

- Beginning to feel "bad" when others hurt
- Sorry might include actual discomfort
- But can't sustain it or really understand it

Around age 6-7: The Empathy Connection

- Can understand others have feelings
- Sorry includes "you feel bad and that makes me feel bad"
- But still struggles with genuine remorse

Around age 8+: Real Remorse

- Understanding of impact on others
- Genuine regret for actions
- Desire to repair relationships
- Sorry becomes meaningful

That's a six-year construction project. Yet we expect a three-year-old to nail it.

The Cultural Sorry Situation

Here's something that makes it even more complex: Different cultures have entirely different sorry universes.

American Sorry: Admission of guilt, personal responsibility

British Sorry: Social lubricant, say it constantly

Japanese Sorry: Complex hierarchy of apologies with physical components

Canadian Sorry: Reflexive, includes apologizing for others' mistakes

If you're raising children in a multicultural household, they're not just learning what sorry means—they're learning multiple incompatible sorry universes. No wonder they're confused.

The Forced Apology Theatre

"You need to apologize to your friend."
"But I'm not sorry!"
"Say it anyway."
"Sorry." (delivered with the enthusiasm of someone reading the phone book)
"Say it like you mean it!"
"SORRY!" (now with jazz hands)

What exactly are we teaching here? That sorry is a performance? That feelings can be faked? That social harmony matters more than honesty?

Maybe. Or maybe we're just hoping that practicing the words will eventually build the feeling. Like doing scales before you can play music.

The Over-Apologizer's Origin Story

Then there's the other extreme. The child who says sorry constantly:

- Sorry for existing
- Sorry for breathing
- Sorry when someone else bumps into them
- Sorry for having needs
- Sorry for feeling feelings

This isn't advanced empathy. This is usually a child who's learned that "sorry" is a protective shield. Say it first, say it often, maybe the big feelings won't come.

The Repair Instead of Sorry Approach

What if, instead of demanding sorry, we taught repair?

Instead of: *"Say sorry for hitting."*
Try: *"Your sister is hurt. What can we do to help her feel better?"*

Instead of: *"Apologize for breaking that."*
Try: *"This is broken now. How can we fix it or replace it?"*

Instead of: *"Say sorry for being mean."*
Try: *"Your friend looks sad. What might help?"*

You're building the universe of repair without requiring the performance of sorry. The word can come later, when it means something.

Try This: The Sorry Detective Game

For one week, track every "sorry" in your house:

- Who says it
- What triggered it
- What happened next
- Did behavior change
- Was anyone actually sorry You might discover:
- Parents say reflexive sorry constantly (modeling meaningless apologies)
- Forced sorries never change behavior
- Natural sorries (when child initiates) are rare but meaningful
- The word has become almost meaningless through overuse

The Universe Construction Project

Building a genuine "sorry" universe takes years and requires:

Emotional awareness: Recognizing own feelings

Empathy development: Understanding others have feelings

Cause-effect understanding: My actions caused those feelings

Remorse capability: Feeling bad about causing bad feelings

Repair motivation: Wanting to fix what was broken

Behavioral control: Ability to not repeat the action

Relationship understanding: Knowing why repair matters

That's seven separate developmental achievements. Most adults struggle with at least three of them. Yet we expect mastery from someone who just learned to use a toilet.

The Compassion Conclusion

So perhaps the next time your child says "SORRY!" while continuing the offensive behavior, instead of frustration, you might feel a tiny bit of wonder.

They're attempting to navigate complex social-emotional universes with a brain that's still figuring out that other people have feelings. They're trying to use words that won't have meaning for years. They're doing their best with the 5% of the universe they can see.

And maybe, just maybe, that cheerful "SORRY!" while still clutching their sister's toy isn't defiance. It's a small human trying to use the magic words you taught them, confused why the spell isn't working like it usually does.

The universe inside "sorry" is vast and complex and takes years to build. Your child isn't refusing to build it. They're just showing you exactly how far they've gotten.

And honestly? For a three-year-old who just learned that other people exist as separate beings with their own thoughts? They're doing pretty well.

PART II

How Children Actually Hear Us

CHAPTER 4

The Comprehension Illusion

Here's a game you can play. Ask a four-year-old to define common words they use every day. Not quiz them—just casually ask "What does 'tomorrow' mean?" or "What is 'angry'?"

The answers will restructure how you think about communication:

- *"Tomorrow is when I wake up"* (but what about naps?)
- *"Angry is when you yell"* (but what about quiet anger?)
- *"Sharing is when you give me things"* (note the direction)
- *"Fast means running"* (but what about fast cars? fast talkers?)
- *"Broken means in pieces"* (but what about broken promises?)

They're not wrong. They're building the universe one star at a time. And sometimes those stars form constellations that look nothing like what we see.

The Vocabulary Illusion

Here's something interesting: Children often use many words they don't fully understand in the adult sense—they really only understand a fraction of those words the way you do.

It's like having a phone with lots of apps where most only partially work, and many do something completely different than what the icon suggests.

> Your child might flawlessly use the word *"actually"* in sentences:
>
> - *"I actually don't want that"*
> - *"Actually, I'm five"*
> - *"That's actually mine"*

Ask them what "actually" means? Crickets. Or maybe "It means... actually?" They've learned the music of the word without understanding the lyrics.

The Great Pretenders

Children are masters of linguistic camouflage. They use context, tone, and adult reactions to fake comprehension constantly.

> Watch a five-year-old in this conversation:
>
> **Adult:** *"We need to be considerate of the neighbors."*
> **Child:** *"Okay!"* (confident nod)
> **Adult:** *"So what does that mean we should do?"*
> **Child:** *"Um... be good?"*
> **Adult:** *"What kind of good?"*
> **Child:** *"The... considerate kind?"*

They're not lying. They're doing what they've learned works: agree, repeat key words, look sincere. It's linguistic survival in a world where adults use words like "considerate" and expect immediate understanding.

The Sensory Foundation of Words

But here's what we miss: Words aren't just sounds with meanings. For children, every word is being built on a foundation of sensory experiences that we've long forgotten we're using.

When you say *"soft,"* your brain instantly accesses:

- The tactile memory of cotton, fur, fleece
- The pressure difference against skin
- The temperature association (soft things are often warm)
- The emotional comfort correlation
- The visual of things that yield when pressed
- Even the sound dampening of soft materials
- That one blanket from childhood (you know the one)

Your four-year-old? They might only have:

- Blankie feels nice
- Mom's voice when she says "soft"
- Maybe clouds look soft? (But they're wet? Confusion.)

That's it. The entire sensory universe you're referencing doesn't exist yet.

The Hot Universe Catastrophe

Watch what happens when sensory universes collide with word universes. A three-year-old learns "hot" from touching a warm bath. Then you say the soup is hot. They blow on it. Good! Then you say "That's a hot color" about a red painting. They literally touch it to check. Then "hot temper." Now they're completely lost.

Then "hot take" on Twitter. Universe explosion.

> The word *"hot"* needs different sensory universes:
>
> - Temperature hot (tactical/pain)
> - Spicy hot (taste/mouth burn)
> - Color hot (visual intensity)
> - Emotion hot (internal sensation)
> - Weather hot (whole body experience)
> - Attractiveness hot (they'll learn this one in middle school)
> - Trending hot (the internet has entered the chat)

Each requires completely different sensory foundations. No wonder they're confused. We're using one word for seven different universes and acting surprised when they check if the red painting burns their hand.

The Sticky Situation

Here's an experiment that will change how you see word learning forever. Watch a two-year-old encounter "sticky" for the first time.

> They touch tape. You say *"sticky."* But what they're actually experiencing:
>
> - Fingers feel pulled
> - Can't let go easily
> - Makes a sound when pulled off
> - Leaves residue on skin
> - Fingers stick together
> - Slightly scary (why won't it come off?)
> - Is this forever? (genuine toddler panic)

Now you say honey is sticky. But honey is:

- Wet (tape wasn't wet)
- Edible (tape definitely wasn't)
- Flows slowly (tape doesn't flow)
- Golden (tape was clear)
- Sweet (no taste to tape)
- Gets on everything (including hair, walls, dog)

In their developing brain, these might be two completely different concepts that happen to share a sound. It will take dozens of "sticky" experiences before they extract the core concept: things that adhere.

And don't even get them started on "sticky situation"— how can a situation be like tape?

The Fast/Slow Paradox

"Hurry up, you're so slow!"
"But I'm running fast!"
"You're still slow!"
"I CAN'T BE FAST AND SLOW!"

Your child has a point. In their universe:

- Fast = moving quickly (running)
- Slow = moving slowly (walking)

They don't understand that:

- Fast relative to the task timeline = still slow
- Running in circles = fast movement but slow progress
- Fast for them ≠ fast for the schedule
- Slow getting ready can include fast individual movements

They're simultaneously fast (their legs) and slow (the overall mission). This paradox breaks their brain because they haven't built the universe where both can be true.

Try This: The Sensory Map

Pick any descriptor word your child "knows." Let's say "rough." Now map their sensory universe:

Ask them:

- *"What things are rough?"*
- *"Show me rough with your hands"*
- *"Does rough have a sound?"*
- *"Can food be rough?"*
- *"Is daddy's face rough?"*
- *"Can a day be rough?"* (watch the confusion)

You'll discover their "rough" universe might only include:

- Tree bark
- Sandpaper
- Maybe daddy's chin

Rough bread? Rough week? Rough draft? Rough estimate? Rough around the edges? Those universes don't exist yet. You might as well be speaking in code.

The Taste-Smell Confusion Convention

Adults know taste and smell are different senses. Children don't. This creates universe collisions we don't even notice.

"This tastes bad," says the five-year-old about medicine. "Just hold your nose," you suggest. They look at you like you've suggested they grow wings.

In their universe:

- Taste happens in the mouth
- Nose is for breathing and occasionally picking
- These are unconnected systems
- You've lost your mind

Or watch them encounter "sour":

- Lemon = sour (taste)
- Sour milk = bad (smell? taste? danger?)
- Sour face = expression (visual)
- Sour mood = angry? (emotional)
- Sour grapes = purple? (wait, that's a metaphor?)

They're trying to build one universe from completely different sensory inputs. The word "sour" means at least five different things requiring different senses, but we act like it's one simple concept.

The Volume Universe

"Use your inside voice."

Seems simple. But consider the sensory universe required:

- Awareness of your own volume (harder than you think)
- Comparison to environmental sound
- Muscle control of vocal cords
- Understanding of space acoustics
- Social awareness of impact on others
- Recognition that "inside" isn't actually about location

A four-year-old literally might not hear the difference between their "inside" and "outside" voice. Their sensory universe for self-produced sound isn't calibrated yet. It's like asking someone to adjust a radio they can't hear.

Plus, they've noticed that sometimes you use your "outside voice" inside (watching sports, stepping on Legos, finding the Sharpie art on the couch). Mixed signals much?

Try This: The Voice Recorder Revelation

Record your child using their "inside voice" and "outside voice." Play it back. Watch their face. Many children are shocked:

"That's not what I sound like!"
"I wasn't THAT loud!"
"My voice is weird!"

They've been operating without accurate sensory feedback about their own volume. It's like finding out you've been wearing your shirt backwards all day.

Now they can build the universe: "Oh, THAT'S what you mean by too loud."

The Temperature Tragedy

"Put on your jacket, it's cold."
"I'm not cold!"
"Yes you are, it's freezing out."
"NO I'M NOT!"
"You'll be cold later!"
"I'M NOT COLD LATER, I'M NOT COLD NOW!"

They're not being difficult. Their sensory universe for temperature is different from yours:

- Higher metabolic rate (they run hotter)
- More active (generating heat)
- Different comfort zones
- Haven't learned to anticipate future cold
- Currently feel fine
- Trust their body more than your weather app

When you say *"it's cold,"* you're referencing:

- Current air temperature
- Wind chill factor
- Anticipated cooling over time
- Social norms about weather-appropriate dress
- Prevention of future discomfort
- That one time you got hypothermia in college

They're referencing:

- I feel fine right now

That's it. The entire predictive sensory universe doesn't exist. They can't feel "future cold" any more than they can taste tomorrow's lunch.

The Texture Disaster

Watch a child have a complete meltdown because their socks "feel wrong." You check— they're the same socks as yesterday. Same brand. Same wash cycle. What happened?

Texture sensitivity fluctuates based on:

- Stress levels
- Tiredness
- Hunger
- Overstimulation
- Mood
- Barometric pressure (really!)
- Whether Jupiter is in retrograde (unconfirmed but suspicious)

Today, those socks feel like sandpaper. Tomorrow, they'll be fine. The sensory universe isn't stable—it shifts based on their internal state. The sock seams that were unnoticeable yesterday are unbearable today because their sensory universe has temporarily reorganized.

And you standing there saying "They're the same socks!" doesn't help because you're right about the socks but wrong about their sensory experience.

The Missing Metaphor and Idiom Universe

"You're walking on thin ice."
(Child looks down at floor)

"That's the last straw!"
(Child: "We have more straws in the drawer.")

"It's raining cats and dogs."
(Child runs to window, disappointed)

"You're driving me up the wall."
(Child: *"You can't drive on walls, that's silly."*)

Metaphors require understanding that words can mean things other than what they literally mean. That's a Level 10 skill when your child is operating at Level 2.

When you say "You're pushing my buttons," they might literally look for buttons. When you say "Money doesn't grow on trees," they might ask which trees you checked. They're not being smart-alecks (yet). They're being literal in a universe where words mean what they mean.

What This Means

The comprehension illusion isn't just about words. It's about the entire sensory foundation those words are built on. When we understand this, "why don't they get it?" transforms into "what sensory universe needs building?"

Every word your child learns isn't just a definition. It's an entire sensory universe that needs construction:

- How it feels
- How it sounds
- How it looks
- How it tastes or smells
- Where it exists in space
- How it changes over time
- What emotions it carries
- Which contexts it applies to

When we get frustrated that they "should know" what a word means, we're forgetting the dozens of sensory experiences we've accumulated to build that understanding.

That *"simple"* word like *"careful"*? It requires:

- Visual (watching for hazards)
- Proprioceptive (controlling body movement)
- Predictive (anticipating consequences)
- Emotional (managing impulses)
- Social (considering impact on others)

Five sensory universes that need to coordinate. No wonder "be careful" doesn't work. You're asking them to activate universes that don't exist yet or can't coordinate.

The child who seems to understand but doesn't follow through? They're not defying you. They're showing you exactly which pieces of the sensory universe they've built and which are still missing.

And honestly? For someone who just recently figured out that they're a separate person from you? They're doing remarkably well.

CHAPTER 5

The Context Problem

Watch what happens when you take a word a child "knows" and move it to a new context.

A five-year-old knows "hot." They use it correctly about soup, about the stove, about summer days. Then you say "That's a hot color" about a red painting. They look at you like you've lost your mind. Touch the painting to check its temperature. Then someone says "hot take" and they're checking if the take has steam coming off it.

Or tell a four-year-old to "wait your turn" at home—they get it. Take them to a busy bakery where "taking a number" is "waiting your turn" and watch the confusion.

"But I AM waiting my turn! I'm standing here!"
"You need to take a number."
"Why do I need a number? I know I'm me!"
"The number tells you when it's your turn."
"But you said wait MY turn, not wait a NUMBER's turn!"

The concept hasn't generalized. It's locked to specific scenarios like apps that only work on one device.

The Angel/Demon Phenomenon

This is why a child can be a perfect angel at school and a chaos agent at home. Parents take this personally.

"If you can behave at school, you can behave at home!"

But here's what's really happening. It's not manipulation (usually). The rules haven't generalized. "Use kind words" at school means:

- Specific phrases teacher taught
- In circle time
- With Mrs. Johnson watching
- Get a sticker
- Move your clip up
- Everyone can see

"Use kind words" at home means:

- ???
- With siblings who know exactly which buttons to push
- No sticker system
- No public accountability
- Mom's too tired to move clips

These aren't the same universe. The connection hasn't been built yet. Your child isn't choosing to be good at school and bad at home. They literally don't understand these are the same expectation.

The Container Problem

For young children, words aren't portable concepts. They're locked in containers:

> **"Quiet"** at library = whisper, walk slowly, gentle with books
> **"Quiet"** at home = stop yelling (maybe)
> **"Quiet"** at church = don't talk at all, also stop wiggling
> **"Quiet"** at movies = can whisper to parent
> **"Quiet"** at bedtime = lay still (but singing okay?)
> **"Quiet"** at restaurant = what do you mean, restaurants are loud?

These aren't the same word to a four-year-old. They're six different words that happen to sound alike. The abstract concept "quiet = reduced volume relative to environment" doesn't exist. Each context has its own universe with its own rules.

Then you wonder why they're using their "library whisper" at home (basically mute) or their "home quiet" at the library (still yelling). They're not being difficult. They're trying to match the right universe to the right container and failing because the filing system doesn't exist yet.

The Person-Locked Universe

Even more confusing: Words can mean different things with different people.

> **"Help"** with Mom: She does it for you while you watch
> **"Help"** with Dad: You hold the flashlight for two hours
> **"Help"** with Teacher: Try first, then ask

"Help" with Grandma: She does everything while telling you you're helping

"Help" with Sibling: Nobody actually helps, you just fight

The same word, five different universes. When a child seems to "know better" with one person but not another, they're not manipulating. They've learned that "help" is person-specific, not concept-general.

This is why:

- They clean up for teacher but not you
- They eat vegetables at grandma's but not home
- They share with friends but not siblings
- They listen to coach but not parent

Each person exists in a different universe with different physics.

The Location Lock

A three-year-old who perfectly uses the potty at home has accidents at the store. Why? "Potty" is location-locked:

Home potty:

- Specific bathroom
- Specific routine
- Specific toilet
- Elmo potty seat
- Step stool
- Mom sings the song

School potty:

- Different height
- Different flush (SO LOUD)
- Different room
- No Elmo
- Teacher doesn't know the song
- Paper towels not normal towels

Store potty:

- Scary hand dryers (sound like jet engines)
- Automatic flush (toilet is alive?!)
- Strange smells
- Echo chamber acoustics
- Mom seems stressed
- Where's the step stool?
- THE TOILET MIGHT EAT ME

Each requires rebuilding the entire universe. The child hasn't generalized "when you feel pressure, find any toilet." They've learned "when you feel pressure at home, go to the home potty." Completely different skill.

Try This: The Context Map

Pick a behavior your child does well in one place but not another. Map the contexts:

Where it works:

- Specific location details
- Who's present
- Time of day
- What comes before/after
- Sensory environment
- Reward/consequence system

Where it doesn't work:

- Different location details
- Different people
- Different time
- Different sequence
- Different sensory input
- Different motivation

You'll see exactly which variables prevent generalization. Now you can build bridges between contexts intentionally instead of just hoping the skill travels.

The Clothing Context Catastrophe

"She dresses herself at school but won't at home!"

At school:

- Everyone dressing simultaneously (social pressure)
- Specific cubby location (spatial anchor)
- Same sequence daily (predictable)
- Timer or song (external structure)
- Praise from teacher (different value than parent praise)
- Friends might see your underwear (motivation!)

At home:

- Dressing alone (no social model)
- Various locations (bed, floor, bathroom, wherever)
- Different sequence (weekday vs weekend)
- No external structure
- Parent assumes competence (less praise)
- Only the dog sees your underwear (dog doesn't care)

The skill hasn't transferred. It exists only in the school universe. It's like knowing how to drive but only in your own car in your own neighborhood.

The Grandparent Phenomenon

"They're perfect angels at Grandma's house!"

Of course they are. Grandma's universe has different physics:

Grandma's Universe:

- Unlimited attention (no competition)
- Novel environment (everything is interesting)
- Special rules (cookies for breakfast? Sure!)
- Different expectations (lower bar)
- Rare occurrence (motivation to maintain)
- Candy appears from pockets (actual magic)
- Bedtime is theoretical
- "No" means "maybe"
- Every toy is amazing because it's "new"

Home Universe:

- Divided attention (stupid baby brother)
- Familiar environment (boring)
- Regular rules (vegetables exist)
- High expectations (you know better!)
- Daily occurrence (no novelty)
- Candy requires negotiation
- Bedtime is enforced (mostly)
- "No" means "no" (after the 5th time)
- Toys are old news

This isn't manipulation. It's context-specific universe activation. The "good behavior" literally doesn't exist in the home universe yet.

The Friend Context Crisis

Watch a child who shares beautifully at school refuse to share at home:

School sharing:

- Teacher-mediated
- Time-limited
- Gets praised
- Socially observed
- Turn timer exists
- Everyone shares so it comes back

Home sharing:

- Parent-assumed
- Indefinite
- Expected not praised
- Sibling-specific
- No timer
- Sibling breaks your stuff

These aren't the same skill. School sharing happens in a universe of external structure. Home sharing requires internal motivation that doesn't exist yet. It's like expecting someone to ref their own soccer game while also playing.

The Restaurant Reality Check

At home, your four-year-old sits nicely at dinner. At a restaurant, they're a disaster. Different universe, different physics:

Home dinner:

- Familiar chair at correct height
- Can get up for potty
- Know how long it takes
- Can see food being made
- Normal sounds and smells
- Can play after

Restaurant dinner:

- Weird chair (might tip!)
- Can't leave table
- Food takes FOREVER
- Can't see kitchen
- So many sounds/smells
- Have to stay even after eating?!

It's not the same experience at all. It's universe vertigo. Like asking someone to perform their normal morning routine in a funhouse.

Building Context Bridges

Instead of expecting automatic generalization, build bridges:

STEP 1: Name the contexts *"At school you share toys. At home we also share toys."*

STEP 2: Find similarities *"Both places have toys. Both places have other kids."*

STEP 3: Acknowledge differences *"At school, teacher helps. At home, mommy helps."*

STEP 4: Practice transfer *"Let's practice school sharing at home."*

STEP 5: Celebrate connection *"You used school sharing at home! Your sharing works everywhere!"*

You're literally building neural pathways between contexts. It's construction work, not magic.

The Time Context Confusion

Morning behavior vs. evening behavior isn't just about tiredness:

Morning universe:
- Fresh brain
- Routine-driven
- Goal-oriented (get to school)
- Hope exists
- Patience reservoir full

Evening universe:
- Depleted brain
- Unstructured
- No clear endpoint
- Hope has left the building
- Patience reservoir has a hole in it

When a child can dress themselves in the morning but not at night, they're not being difficult. The evening universe doesn't have the same structural supports. It's like expecting someone to navigate in the dark using their morning memory of the room.

The Car Catastrophe

"He's fine at home but has meltdowns in the car!"

HOME: Can move, multiple rooms, their stuff, escape routes

CAR: Strapped down, tiny space, limited items, NO ESCAPE

The car is a context prison. Same child, different physics. The meltdown isn't defiance—it's universe claustrophobia.

What This Means

Every context requires rebuilding understanding. That's exhausting for little brains. Imagine having to relearn how to walk every time you entered a new room.

When we understand context lock:

- We stop saying "you know better"
- We build bridges between contexts
- We celebrate each successful transfer
- We recognize the exhaustion of constant translation

The child who "knows better" but doesn't do better isn't defying you. They know better in a different universe. The knowledge hasn't traveled yet.

They're not being inconsistent. They're being exactly as consistent as their context-locked understanding allows. And honestly? For someone navigating dozens of different universes every day? They're doing remarkably well.

Your job isn't to be frustrated that the skill doesn't transfer. It's to help them build bridges between universes. One context at a time. One bridge at a time. One patient (or semi-patient, we're all human) moment at a time.

CHAPTER 6

The Speed of Thought Problem

Research suggests children process language at roughly half the speed of adults, though individual variation is significant. When they're tired? Maybe less. When they're hungry? You might as well be speaking to a houseplant.

But we don't slow down. We just get louder.

"Clean your room, brush your teeth, get your backpack, don't forget your lunch, and hurry up we're late!"

Five instructions. Delivered in three seconds. The child is still processing "clean" when you've hit "late." Then we wonder why they're standing there looking blank, one sock on, holding a toothbrush, eating their lunch.

It's not defiance. It's buffer overflow. Their brain just blue-screened.

The Morning Rush Massacre

Let's map a typical morning in slow motion:

7:00 AM: *"Time to wake up, we need to get dressed, eat breakfast, brush teeth, and get to school!"*

What parent thinks they said: Here's our morning plan

What child's brain is processing: Time... to... wake... [BUFFERING]

7:05 AM: *"Why aren't you dressed yet?!"*

Child's brain: Still processing "wake up." Wait, there was more? Dressed? What?

7:10 AM: *"HURRY UP! GET DRESSED! FIND YOUR SHOES! WHERE'S YOUR BACKPACK? DID YOU BRUSH YOUR TEETH?"*

Child's brain: ERROR ERROR ERROR ERROR ERROR SYSTEM OVERLOAD INITIATE CRYING.EXE

7:15 AM: Child is naked, crying, one shoe on wrong foot, eating toothpaste.

Parent: *"WHY DON'T YOU LISTEN?!"*

Child: [Brain has left the chat]

The Processing Bottleneck

Imagine your child might be like a computer from 1995 trying to stream Netflix. Each word has to:

1. **Enter through ears** (sound waves)
2. **Convert to meaning** (auditory processing)
3. **Access word universe** (memory retrieval)
4. **Connect to context** (current situation)
5. **Generate response** (action planning)
6. **Execute action** (motor control)

Adults do this in milliseconds. Children need seconds. SECONDS. While you're already three sentences ahead, they're still trying to figure out if "clean" means "put things away" or "wash with soap" or "make it look nice" or that one time you said "clean" but meant "hide everything before grandma comes."

The Multiplication Disaster

Here's what makes it worse. Multiple instructions don't add—they multiply in complexity:

One instruction: *"Get your shoes"*
- Processing load: 1x
- Success rate: 80%
- Time to complete: 2 minutes

Two instructions: *"Get your shoes and socks"*
- Processing load: 3x (hold first while processing second)
- Success rate: 60%
- Time to complete: 5 minutes

Three instructions: *"Get your shoes, socks, and coat"*
- Processing load: 7x (juggling multiple while processing new)
- Success rate: 30%
- Time to complete: 10 minutes (includes meltdown)

Four instructions: *"Get your shoes, socks, coat, and backpack"*
- Processing load: 15x (system overload)
- Success rate: 5%
- Time to complete: Never. Child is now playing with dog.

Five instructions: [Child.exe has stopped responding. Would you like to restart?]

The Speed Test Reality

Try This: The Family Speed Experiment

Record yourself giving normal-speed instructions to your child. Then play it back at half speed. THAT'S closer to how fast they're processing.

It sounds like this in their brain: "Geeeeeet yooooouuuur shooooooeeees aaaaaand..." (Meanwhile, you've already moved on to discussing world peace and tax returns)

Now try this for a week:

- **Monday:** Normal speed instructions (chaos)
- **Tuesday:** 75% speed (slightly less chaos)
- **Wednesday:** 50% speed (Mr. Rogers pace—we'll talk about him in a moment)
- **Thursday:** 50% speed with pauses (magic happens)
- **Friday:** Track compliance rate (prepare to be amazed)

Most families see compliance jump from 30% to 80% just by slowing down. It's not that your child wasn't listening. They literally couldn't process at your speed.

The Mr. Rogers Secret

Fred Rogers seemed to speak at a deliberately slower pace—and parents consistently noticed their children paid attention to him differently than to faster-talking adults. Whatever the exact speed, something about that measured pace seemed to work.

That wasn't just an aesthetic choice—it appears to have been intentional:

- Slow enough for children to process
- Pauses between thoughts
- Single-concept sentences
- Repetition of key words
- Time for visual processing
- Never rushed, never overwhelming

He wasn't talking down to children. He seemed to understand something about synchronizing with their processing speed. Whether he knew the neuroscience or just intuitively understood children's needs, the result was the same: children could actually follow along.

The Question Collision

"Do you want oatmeal or eggs for breakfast and did you brush your teeth yet and where are your shoes?"

Three questions. Zero answers. Here's why:

Question 1 arrives → Brain starts processing

Question 2 arrives → Abandons Q1, starts Q2

Question 3 arrives → Abandons Q2, starts Q3

Result: Blank stare, possibly drooling

The child isn't ignoring you. Their processor is stuck in a restart loop. It's like trying to open seventeen browser tabs on a computer from 2003. Everything freezes, nothing works, and somehow the printer starts making noises.

The Interrupt Catastrophe

Many children find it difficult to pause processing like adults can.
When you interrupt their thinking:

Adult brain: Pause current thought → Process interruption →
Resume

Child brain: ABANDON EVERYTHING → Start over →
Forget what I was doing → Why am I holding a banana?

"What do you want for—oh, did you feed the dog?
Anyway, what do you want for lunch?"

The child was building "lunch" universe. You destroyed it with
"dog." Now they can't remember what they were thinking about.
They're holding a banana. Are they feeding the dog a banana?
Having banana for lunch? Why are you talking about dogs?
Meltdown incoming.

The Translation Lag

Even when children understand, there's a translation lag:

Hear instruction → Decode words → Understand
meaning → Plan action → Execute

Adult: 1-2 seconds total
Around 3-year-old: 5-10 seconds
Around 5-year-old: 3-5 seconds
Around 7-year-old: 2-3 seconds
Teenager: Heard you but choosing to ignore (different problem)

But we rarely wait. We repeat, rephrase, or add more instructions during their processing time, creating chaos:

"Put on your shoes." (2 seconds pass)

"I said shoes!" (Child was mid-processing, now restarting)

"SHOES! ON YOUR FEET!" (Child crying, no shoes,
possibly eating shoes)

The Noise Competition

In a quiet room, a child processes at their maximum rate. Add noise:

- **TV on:** Processing drops 30%
- **Sibling talking:** Processing drops 40%
- **Multiple conversations:** Processing drops 60%
- **Dog barking:** Processing drops 70%
- **Stressed/yelling parent:** Processing drops 80%
- **Sibling singing Baby Shark:** Processing drops 100%, parent's processing also drops 100%

That instruction you're shouting over the TV, while their sibling is singing, as the dog barks? They're getting maybe 20% of it. The other 80% is just mouth movements and angry faces.

Try This: The Silent Start

Tomorrow morning, try 10 minutes of no talking. Use:

- Gestures
- Pointing
- Demonstration
- Interpretive dance if necessary

Watch how much smoother everything goes when their processor isn't overloaded with words.

The End-of-Day Collapse

Processing speed deteriorates throughout the day like a phone battery with too many apps open:

> **7 AM:**   **75 words per minute** (if fully awake)
>
> **12 PM:**   **60 words per minute** (lunch helps temporarily)
>
> **3 PM:**   **50 words per minute** (why is afternoon so long?)
>
> **6 PM:**   **40 words per minute** (dinner zombie mode)
>
> **8 PM:**   **25 words per minute** (why aren't you in bed?)
>
> **9 PM:**   **10 words per minute** (child is basically furniture)

That bedtime instruction that seems simple? Their processor is running at 30% capacity. No wonder bedtime is a battle. You're asking a nearly-dead phone to run Photoshop.

The Emotional Processor Drain

Strong emotions hijack processing power:

> **EXCITED:** Processing drops 40% (too much energy elsewhere)
> *"We're going to Disney World!"*
> *"YAY! Wait, what? Where? When? DISNEY!"*
> (Understanding: 10%)
>
> **ANGRY:** Processing drops 60% (fight/flight taking resources)
> *"I'M MAD!"*
> *"Use your words to tell me why."*
> *"WORDS! MAD! LOUD NOISES!"*

SAD: Processing drops 50% (emotional processing priority)

Sobbing *"But... I... wanted... the... blue... cup..."*

"The blue cup is in the dishwasher."

"...what's a dishwasher?"

SCARED: Processing drops 70% (survival mode activated)

"There's a monster!"

"No monsters here, time for bed."

"BED IS WHERE MONSTERS LIVE!"

"I TOLD YOU TO CLEAN UP!" yelled at an upset child processes as: "... TOLD ... CLEAN ..." The rest is lost to emotional static.

The Sibling Speed Differential

When you have multiple kids, you're broadcasting at different required speeds:

To the 8-year-old: Normal speed fine

To the 5-year-old: Need 75% speed

To the 2-year- old: Need 40% speed

To all three at once: Nobody understands anything

"Everyone get ready for bed!"

- 8-year-old starts moving
- 5-year-old heard "everyone" and "bed"
- 2-year-old heard sounds and likes sounds

This is why individual instructions work better than group announcements. You're not being inefficient. You're matching processing speeds.

Building Processing Bridges

The Chunk Method:

Instead of:
"Go upstairs, brush your teeth, put on pajamas, and pick a book"
Try:
"Go upstairs." [Wait for completion]
"Now brush teeth." [Wait]
"Now pajamas." [Wait]
"Pick a book." [Success!]

The Echo Check:

"What did I just ask you to do?"
Not *"Did you hear me?"* (they'll always say yes) Their translation
reveals what actually processed:

You: *"Clean up and get ready for dinner."*
Child: *"Dinner!"*
You: (Now you know what registered)

The Visual Support:

- Point while speaking
- Demonstrate while explaining
- Draw simple pictures
- Use fingers to count steps
- Make silly faces for emphasis

Visual processing is faster than auditory for many children. When
words fail, try interpretive dance. Your dignity is already gone
anyway.

The Speed of Different Words

Not all words process at the same speed:

Fast processing: Concrete nouns (shoe, cookie, dog)

Medium processing: Action verbs (run, eat, sleep)

Slow processing: Abstract concepts (behave, consider, appreciate)

Glacial processing: Emotional words (disappointed, frustrated, overwhelmed)

Never processes: "We'll see" (might as well be speaking in tongues)

When you use slow-processing words at high speed, it's like trying to download a movie on dial-up while someone's using the phone.

The Patience Paradox

Here's the cruel irony: The times children most need slow, clear instructions are when we're least able to provide them:

Morning rush: Need slow speech, parent stressed and speeding up

Bedtime: Need patient repetition, parent exhausted

Getting out door: Need calm clarity, already 10 minutes late

Homework time: Need processing space, parent has 47 other things to do

We speed up when we need to slow down. We get louder when we need to get clearer. We add instructions when we need to subtract them.

What This Means

When a child "doesn't listen," they might be:

- Still processing instruction #1 of your 5-instruction combo
- Overwhelmed by speed
- Lost in translation lag
- Processor-blocked by noise
- Running on depleted resources
- Trying to decode why you're doing interpretive dance

Slowing down isn't dumbing down. It's syncing up. You're not accommodating weakness—you're respecting neurology.

The child standing there looking blank while you repeat instructions louder and faster? They're not defying you. They're buffering. Their little processor is doing its best with hardware that won't be fully upgraded for another 20 years.

And maybe, just maybe, if we all channeled just a little bit more of that Mr. Rogers pace (if you're not already)- that gentle, deliberate way of speaking that seemed to assume children were worth taking time for—we'd find that our children aren't bad at listening.

They're just operating at a different speed. And that's okay. Even if it means breakfast takes 47 minutes and you're late for everything forever.

PART III

Emotional Worlds

CHAPTER 7

Emotional Universes

A six-year-old comes home from school. *"Jake was mean."*

Parent launches into: *"Well, how do you think Jake felt? Maybe he was having a hard day. You should try to be understanding. Remember when you were upset and said things you didn't mean? We all have bad days sometimes..."*

The parent is operating in an emotional universe that includes theory of mind, emotional complexity, empathy as action, and social repair strategies.

The child meant: *"Jake took my crayon."*

That's it. "Mean" equals "did something I didn't like." The emotional universe of considering Jake's internal state while processing their own disappointment while planning future social strategies? That universe doesn't exist yet. It's like asking someone to write a symphony when they just learned "Hot Cross Buns" on the recorder.

The Body-First Universe

What if before a child can understand "frustrated," they have to experience:

- The chest tightening
- The jaw clenching
- The urge to throw something
- The heat rising in their face
- The almost-crying-but-not-quite
- The wanting-but-can't-having
- That specific growl that comes from nowhere
- The sudden hatred of everything, especially socks

These aren't symptoms of frustration. What if for a child, they ARE frustration. What if the body teaches the brain the emotion, not the other way around.

Watch a three-year-old get frustrated. Do they say "I'm frustrated." Or do they:

- Throw themselves on the floor
- Make dinosaur sounds
- Clench their entire body
- Hit something (or someone, or themselves, or the dog)
- Become a tornado of limbs
- Somehow end up under the couch

If they're not being dramatic. They could be literally experiencing the emotion through their whole body because maybe the abstract concept hasn't formed yet. What if the body IS the emotion. What if they're not having a feeling – What if they're BEING a feeling.

Try This: The Emotion Detective

Next time your child has a big feeling, don't name it immediately. Instead, be a body detective:

> *"I see your hands are making fists."*
>
> *"Your face is getting red."*
>
> *"Your voice got louder."*
>
> *"Your body wants to move fast."*
>
> *"You're making that growling sound."*
>
> *"You just threw yourself backward for no apparent reason."*
>
> Then connect:
>
> *"When our body does all those things, that feeling is called angry."*

You're building the universe from the body up, not the word down. Plus, narrating their breakdown like a nature documentary sometimes makes you both laugh, which helps.

The Contagion Universe

What if children catch emotions like colds. Not metaphorically—literally.

When you're anxious, your child's body starts producing stress hormones within minutes. They don't know why. They just suddenly feel bad. When you say "I'm stressed but you don't need to worry," their body is already worried. The words are meaningless against the biochemical reality.

It's like telling someone "Don't smell this" while holding a skunk directly under their nose. Have you ever noticed that:

- They melt down when you're rushing (they caught your urgency)
- They can't sleep when you're anxious (cortisol is contagious)
- They act out when you're angry at someone else (the anger leaked)
- They get hyperactive when you're excited (emotional overflow)
- They have a meltdown right when you're on an important call (they sense your tension and express it for you)

A four-year-old in a stressed household may not be "acting out." They may be drowning in emotions that aren't even theirs, without words to explain what's happening. Perhaps they're emotional sponges in an anxiety ocean.

The Measurement Problem

"How are you feeling?"
"Fine."
"No really, how are you feeling?"
"I SAID FINE!"
"But you're crying."
"FINE!"

They're not being difficult. What if "Fine" is the only measurement they have. Asking for more nuance would be like asking them to describe colors that don't exist.

Adult emotional measurements:
- Slightly annoyed → Irritated → Frustrated → Angry → Furious → Volcanic
- Concerned → Worried → Anxious → Panicked → Full existential crisis
- Content → Happy → Joyful → Ecstatic → Transcendent bliss

Child emotional measurements (around age 4):
- Good
- Bad
- Mad
- VERY mad (new category discovered through experience)

That's it. Four settings. You're asking for a dimmer switch when they only have on/off/explosion/nuclear.

The Yesterday Feelings Problem

"Remember how you felt when Sophie wouldn't share?"
Blank stare.

"Yesterday? At the park? You were so upset?"
Still blank.

"You cried for twenty minutes?"
"I want a snack."

Children under six struggle with remember feelings. They can remember events. They can remember what happened. But the feeling itself? Probably gone. Evaporated. Deleted from the hard drive.

Some research suggests:
- They repeat behaviors that made them miserable yesterday
- They can't learn from emotional experiences
- *"Remember how sad you were?"* doesn't work as deterrent
- They need the same comfort for the same problem repeatedly
- They're genuinely surprised by the same feelings every time

When you reference past emotions, you're asking them to access a universe that evaporates the moment the feeling passes. It's like asking them to remember being asleep or describe what it felt like to not exist before they were born.

The Jealousy Galaxy

Jealousy might be the most complex emotional universe a child has to build. It requires:

- Theory of mind (understanding others have things/experiences)
- Comparison (more/less/same)
- Desire projection (I want what they have)
- Social understanding of fairness
- Time comprehension (they got more yesterday)
- Self-awareness (I want what they have)
- Future projection (will I get it too?)
- Mathematical skills (their cookie is 0.02% bigger)

At around four-years-old when they says "That's not fair!" about a sibling's cookie being imperceptibly larger, they're attempting to navigate eight different universes simultaneously. No wonder they melt down.

But here's what makes jealousy even more complex—it can be physically uncomfortable. Brain scans show social rejection and unfairness activate the same regions as physical pain. Some research suggests when a child sees a sibling get something they don't, they may actually feel discomfort. They're not being dramatic.

"My tummy hurts!"

"You just saw your sister get a sticker."

"AND MY TUMMY HURTS!"

Both are true. The sticker caused physical discomfort. Try explaining that to grandma.

The Shame Spiral

Shame is different from all other emotions because it attacks the self, not the situation. And children don't have enough "self" built yet to withstand it.

Some research suggests when a five-year-old experiences shame:

- Their entire universe collapses to one thought:
  "I'm bad"
- Not "I did something bad"—that requires separation of self from action
- Just *"I'm bad"*—total, complete, existential
- Everything is bad
- They've always been bad
- They'll always be bad
- Maybe they should live under the bed now

This is why shame-based discipline backfires so spectacularly. You think you're teaching them not to hit. Perhaps instead they're learning to think they're fundamentally broken. The lesson you're teaching and the universe they're building have nothing to do with each other.

The Mixed Feelings Paradox

"I love my sister but I also hate her right now."

A seven-year-old can't hold these two truths simultaneously. Their emotional universe is binary. You love OR you hate. Happy OR sad. Good OR bad.

What if when they experience mixed feelings, their brain doesn't have the architecture to process both. So it picks one, usually the strongest or most recent. This is why they can go from "I hate you!" to "I love you!" in seconds. They're not lying either time. Their brain just can't hold both truths together yet.

It's like trying to run two operating systems at once on a computer that can barely handle solitaire.

Try This: The Both/And Bridge

When you see mixed feelings emerging:

> *"Your face looks happy but your voice sounds sad."*
>
> *"Part of you wants to go and part wants to stay."*
>
> *"You love your friend AND you're mad at them."*
>
> *"You're excited about the party AND scared about the new kids."*

Use "AND" not "BUT." You're building neural pathways that can hold complexity. Each "and" is a bridge between emotional universes that couldn't touch before.

Expect confused face, possible shutdown, requests for snacks.

The Empathy Ladder

Parents think empathy is one thing. It's actually five different universes that build in order:

LEVEL 1—Emotional Contagion (birth to around-2):
Crying when others cry (emotion virus)

LEVEL 2—Emotional Recognition (around 2-4):
"He's sad" (can identify face)

LEVEL 3—Emotional Understanding (around 4-6):
"He's sad because his toy broke" (cause and effect)

LEVEL 4—Emotional Perspective (around 6-8): *"He's sad even though I wouldn't be"* (different people, different feelings)

LEVEL 5—Emotional Action (around 8+): *"He's sad so I'll help"* (empathy becomes behavior)

When you ask a four-year-old to "think about how your friend feels," you're asking them to skip to Level 4. They're still on Level 2. They can see the friend is sad. They can't understand why or what to do about it. It's like asking them to solve calculus when they're still counting on fingers.

The Emotional Weather Report

Children's emotions change like weather, except faster and more dramatically:

7:00 AM:	**Sunny** (happy about everything)
7:03 AM:	**Thunderstorm** (wrong spoon)
7:05 AM:	**Rainbow** (found correct spoon)
7:07 AM:	**Tornado** (sibling exists)
7:10 AM:	**Partly cloudy** (distracted by dog)
7:12 AM:	**Hurricane** (time to get dressed)

What if you're not dealing with moods. You're dealing with rapid weather systems moving through a tiny body. The forecast is always: unpredictable with a chance of meltdown.

The Comfort Object Universe

That ratty stuffed animal your child can't sleep without? It's not just a toy. It's an entire emotional universe:

- Safety when scared
- Consistency when everything changes
- Control when powerless
- Comfort when sad
- Friend when lonely
- Piece of home when away
- Container for all feelings
- Therapist who never judges
- The one thing that's truly theirs

When you say "It's just a toy, we'll wash it," you're not understanding. What if that bunny holds their entire emotional support system. Washing it is like reformatting their emotional hard drive.

This is why losing it causes complete breakdown. It's not about the object. It's about losing their emotional universe anchor. It's existential crisis in stuffed animal form.

The Repair Universe

"Say sorry and mean it."

We've covered why "sorry" is empty. But "meaning it" requires understanding repair—that relationships can break and be fixed, that actions have lasting impacts, that trust is a thing that exists.

Around four-years-old their relationship universe resets every few minutes:

- Mad at mom (8:00)
- Love mom (8:03)
- Mad at mom (8:07)
- Love mom (8:10)
- Snack? (8:11)

There's nothing to repair because nothing stays broken. Each interaction is a new universe, unconnected to the last. This is why they:

- Can hit their friend then immediately want to play
- Don't understand why you're "still" mad
- Can't comprehend "lost trust"
- Think "sorry" fixes everything instantly
- Are genuinely confused by grudges

The concept that relationships have continuity, that they accumulate damage and repair over time—that's an emotional universe that won't fully form until around age 8 or later.

The Love Language Confusion

"I love you more than..." games reveal how children understand love:

Around age 3: *"I love you more than... cookies!"* (highest compliment possible)

Around age 4: *"I love you more than infinity!"* (just learned this word)

Around age 5: *"I love you more than all the stars!"* (poetry phase)

Around age 6: *"I love you more than video games!"* (actually meaningful)

Around age 7: *"I love you... I guess"* (too cool phase beginning)

They're not being cute. They're trying to quantify an emotion using whatever measurement system they have. Usually food-based.

What This Means

The emotional universe is the most complex universe children build. Every feeling requires:

- Body awareness
- Language for sensation
- Cause-effect understanding
- Memory of similar feelings
- Social context
- Appropriate expression
- Regulation strategies

When a child has an emotional meltdown, what if they're not being manipulative or dramatic. What if they're experiencing universe collapse without words to explain it, without tools to fix it, without understanding of why it's happening.

Your frustration when they can't "just calm down"? Justified. Their inability to calm down? Also justified. You're both right. You're both struggling. You're both doing your best with the emotional universes you have available.

And maybe that's the most important emotional universe to build—the one where everyone's feelings are real, even when we don't understand them, even when they're inconvenient, even when they're about the wrong spoon at 7:03 AM.

Because someday, that child who melted down over the blue cup will be a teenager telling you their heart is broken. And you'll remember: feelings don't have to make sense to be real. The universe inside them is valid, even when we can't see it from the outside.

CHAPTER 8

The Abstraction Ladder

Here's something adults do without thinking: We climb up and down the abstraction ladder all day.

"Be good" (abstract)

"Share your toys" (less abstract)

"Give Sarah the truck" (concrete)

For adults, these are the same instruction at different resolutions, like zooming in and out on Google Maps. For children, they're completely different languages. Like asking someone to navigate using a street map, a subway map, and a constellation chart simultaneously.

A four-year-old can follow "Give Sarah the truck." They cannot follow "Be considerate of others' feelings." The neural pathways that connect concrete actions to abstract concepts are still under construction. Like asking someone to use an elevator in a building where only the stairs have been built. And half the stairs are missing. And some lead to nowhere. And occasionally they're made of Jello.

The Ladder Levels

Let's map the abstraction ladder from concrete to abstract:

LEVEL 1—Physical/Immediate: *"Pick up the red block"*
- Specific object, specific action
- Can see and touch
- Immediate execution
- Success rate: 90%

LEVEL 2—Categorical/Simple: *"Pick up the blocks"*
- Category of objects
- Still visible
- Clear action
- Success rate: 70%
- (Warning: May pick up one block and declare victory)

LEVEL 3—Conceptual/Basic: *"Clean up your toys"*
- Multiple categories
- Requires decisions
- Implied endpoint
- Success rate: 40%
- (Everything might end up in one pile)

LEVEL 4—Abstract/Complex: *"Keep your room tidy"*
- Ongoing state
- Multiple components
- Subjective standard
- Success rate: 15%
- (What's "tidy"? Is under the bed tidy?)

LEVEL 5—Philosophical/Values: *"Be responsible for your space"*
- Abstract concept
- No specific actions
- Value system required
- Success rate: 0%
- (Child.exe has encountered an error and needs to close)

A three-year-old operates at Level 1-2. You're speaking at Level 4-5. No wonder there's confusion. It's like giving GPS coordinates to someone who doesn't know what numbers are.

The Good Child Paradox

"Be good" might be the most useless instruction ever given to children. Let's unpack what "good" requires understanding:

- Social expectations (varies by context)
- Behavioral inhibition (stop wants)
- Emotional regulation (manage feelings)
- Future prediction (consequences)
- Value alignment (match adult priorities)
- Sustained performance (ongoing, not momentary)
- Mind reading (what does THIS adult consider good?)
- Weather patterns (apparently being good depends on barometric pressure)

To a four-year-old, "be good" means... nothing. Or everything. Or maybe "don't do the thing that made mom mad yesterday." But today is a new day with new physics. Yesterday's "good" might be today's "why are you just sitting there?"

Try This: The Good Detective

Ask your child: "What does 'be good' mean?" Common answers:

- *"Don't be bad"* (circular logic)
- *"Be quiet"* (one specific interpretation)
- *"I don't know"* (honest)
- *"Listen to mommy"* (still abstract)
- *"No hitting"* (oddly specific)
- *"Eat vegetables?"* (confused guess)
- *"Not like yesterday"* (remembers consequences)

Now build it concretely: "Being good at the store means: Hold my hand, walking feet, inside voice, hands to yourself, no asking for things, no licking the cart handle, no hiding in the clothing racks, no opening packages, no free samples without asking, no crawling under displays..."

(List continues for 47 more items.)

You've translated Level 5 abstraction to Level 1 concrete actions. Congratulations, you've written a novel.

The Sharing Catastrophe

"Share" is an abstraction that contains multitudes:

LEVEL 5: *"Be generous with others"*
Translation: ???

LEVEL 4: *"Share your things"*
Translation: Give away everything I love?

LEVEL 3: *"Let others have turns"*
Translation: But when is my turn again?

LEVEL 2: *"Give some to your brother"*
Translation: How much is some? One crumb?

LEVEL 1: *"Put one car in Tommy's hand"*
Translation: Finally, instructions I can follow! *Throws car at Tommy's face*

When you say "share," you're at Level 4. The child hears noise. When you say "Put one car in Tommy's hand gently," they can comply. Same goal, different ladder rung, less facial injury.

The Kindness Confusion

Watch the abstraction ladder fail in real-time:

Parent: *"Be kind to your sister"*
Child: [Blank stare]

Parent: *"Use nice words"*
Child: *"Hi sister!"* [Then hits her]

Parent: "Gentle touches"
Child: [Pats head really hard]

Parent: *"Pat softly like this"*
Child: [Finally succeeds]

Parent: [Exhausted from climbing down ladder]

Four attempts to descend from abstract to concrete. Each level confused the child more. By the end, everyone's frustrated, sister has a headache, and "kindness" has lost all meaning.

The School Success Mystery

Why do children follow complex instructions at school but not at home? Teachers unconsciously use the abstraction ladder:

> *"Class, we're going to clean up"*
> (Level 4—announcement)
>
> *"When I clap, start cleaning"*
> (Level 3—trigger)
>
> *"Blocks in the blue bin"*
> (Level 2—category)
>
> *"Sam, put that block here"*
> (Level 1—specific)
>
> *"No, Sam, here. HERE. This spot. Right here Sam."*

They scaffold down the ladder for each child's developmental level. Parents often stay at Level 4-5, wondering why nothing happens, speaking to the clouds while their child needs ground-level directions.

The Emotion Abstraction Disaster

> *"Control yourself!"* (Level 5)
> **Child:** Continues melting down
>
> *"Calm down!"* (Level 4)
> **Child:** Melting intensifies
>
> *"Stop crying!"* (Level 3)
> **Child:** Now screaming
>
> *"Take deep breaths!"* (Level 2)
> **Child:** Hyperventilating
>
> *"Breathe in... now out..."* (Level 1)
> **Child:** Finally starting to regulate

A melting-down child can only access Level 1. Everything above that is noise. Yet we usually start at Level 5 and get frustrated when it doesn't work. It's like yelling philosophical concepts at someone who's drowning instead of throwing them a rope.

The Future Abstraction Problem

Abstract concepts often involve future thinking:

"Be prepared" = Imagine future state, work backward
"Save your money" = Deny present for future benefit
"Think ahead" = Simulate scenarios that don't exist
"Plan your day" = Organize time that hasn't happened
"Study for the test" = Learn things for future demonstration

Children under 6 can barely imagine tomorrow, much less abstract future states. "Be prepared" is meaningless. "Pack your backpack now" is actionable. One requires time travel, the other requires putting objects in a bag.

The Responsibility Rubik's Cube

"Be responsible" might be the ultimate abstraction. Let's unpack it:

What adults mean:
- Complete tasks without reminders
- Anticipate needs
- Consider consequences
- Maintain possessions
- Follow through on commitments
- Demonstrate maturity
- Make good choices
- Be trustworthy
- Show initiative
- Basically become a tiny adult

What child understands:

- That word mom says
- Something about cleaning?
- I'm in trouble

The gap between these universes is astronomical. You might as well ask them to understand cryptocurrency or explain why adults watch the news.

The Behavior Abstraction Breakdown

"Behave yourself!"

This instruction assumes:

- Child knows what behavior is expected
- In this specific context
- With these specific people
- At this specific time
- And can execute it
- Consistently
- Without support
- While managing emotions
- And sensory input
- And social dynamics

That's ten simultaneous calculations. Your child is still trying to figure out if they need to pee.

Try This: The Three-Level Rule

Whatever instruction you want to give, create three versions:

LEVEL 5 (your thought): *"Be considerate"*
LEVEL 3 (simplified): *"Think about others"*
LEVEL 1 (actionable): *"Ask Sam if he wants a turn"*

Always end at Level 1 for action, but include higher levels for learning. Like teaching a language—you speak simply but don't baby talk.

The Manners Mountain

"Have good manners" is an abstraction containing infinite smaller abstractions:

- Say please (when?)
- Say thank you (for what?)
- Don't interrupt (but I need to pee)
- Chew with mouth closed (physically difficult)
- Napkin on lap (why?)
- Elbows off table (but my arms are tired)
- Wait to be excused (imprisoned by furniture)
- Make eye contact (but not too much)
- Firm handshake (what's firm?)
- Inside voice (which inside?)

Each "manner" is its own universe requiring separate construction. "Good manners" is asking them to juggle twenty universes while eating soup. No wonder they end up wearing it.

The Honesty Hilarity

"Always tell the truth" seems simple until:

"Do you like grandma's cooking?"

"No, it's gross!"

"That's rude!"

"But you said tell the truth!"

Now you're explaining white lies, social grace, kindness versus honesty, context-appropriate truth, and why grandma is crying. The "simple" instruction to be honest just became a philosophy course.

The Trying Trap

"Just try your best!"

What is "best"? How do you measure trying? What if my best is terrible? What if I tried but you can't see it? What if my best changes by minute? What if trying makes me tired? What if...

"Just write your name on the paper."

"OH. Okay."

Sometimes the abstraction ladder needs to be a slide straight to the bottom.

Building Abstraction Bridges

The Ladder Method:

Start abstract (for you): **"Be responsible"**

Climb down:

- "Take care of your things"
- "Put things where they belong"
- "Toys go in the toy box"
- "Put this bear in that box"

Now climb back up:

- "Good! You put bear away"
- "You put toys where they belong"
- "You took care of your things"
- "That's being responsible!"

You're building neural pathways between levels. It takes approximately 847 repetitions.

The Development Timeline

Age 2-3: Levels 1-2 only

- Concrete, immediate, visible
- "Give cookie" works
- "Be generous" doesn't

Age 4-5: Level 3 emerging

- Simple categories, basic concepts
- "Clean up toys" works
- "Maintain order" doesn't

Age 6-7: Level 4 developing

- Abstract concepts with support
- "Be helpful" starting to work
- "Show initiative" still doesn't

Age 8-10: Level 5 beginning

- Values and philosophy with lots of examples
- "Be responsible" gaining meaning
- "Actualize your potential" still nonsense

Age 11+: Full ladder access

- Can translate between levels
- Understands metaphor
- Still thinks adults are weird

The Homework Abstraction

"Do your homework" (Level 4)

Requires understanding:

- Future obligations
- Task prioritization
- Time management
- Self-direction
- Quality standards
- The point of homework (nobody understands this)

Versus:

"Sit at table, open math book, do problem 1" (Level 1) Same goal, accessible instruction, less existential crisis.

What This Means

When children don't follow abstract instructions, they're not being defiant. They're being asked to operate at an abstraction level their brain can't reach yet.

It's like being frustrated that someone on the first floor can't reach something on the fifth floor. The elevator hasn't been built yet. The stairs are under construction. They're not refusing to go up— there's literally no way up.

Understanding the abstraction ladder transforms communication:

- Start concrete, build abstract
- Always provide Level 1 option
- Celebrate when they climb levels
- Stop expecting Level 5 from Level 2 brains

The child who can't "be good"? They need you to climb down the ladder and meet them where they are. Then, and only then, can you help them climb up.

One concrete step at a time. One specific instruction at a time. One exhausted parent at a time.

And maybe, just maybe, by the time they're teenagers, they'll understand "be responsible." But they still won't understand why you watch the news.

CHAPTER 9

The Social Universe

"Be nice to your sister."

Seems simple. But "nice" requires:

- Reading her emotional state
- Predicting what would please her
- Suppressing your own desires
- Understanding relationship maintenance
- Navigating power dynamics
- Managing jealousy
- Projecting future consequences
- Remembering she's the one who broke your LEGO yesterday
- Forgetting she's the one who broke your LEGO yesterday
- Somehow doing both simultaneously

The child's version of "nice": Don't hit her. Maybe. For the next five minutes. Unless she looks at me. Or breathes too loud. Or exists in my space.

We're asking them to navigate social complexities that took us decades to understand (and let's be honest, we still mess up regularly). It's like expecting a tourist to navigate your city like a local, except the tourist is three feet tall and thinks everyone is out to steal their goldfish crackers.

The Playground Politics

The playground is a masterclass in social universe collision. Watch a four-year-old navigate:

The Swing Situation:

- Someone's on the swing they want
- "Sharing" means taking turns
- But how long is a turn?
- Who decides?
- What if they never get off?
- Is pushing them off "not nice"?
- But waiting forever isn't fair?
- Maybe crying will help?
- Crying didn't help
- Now everyone's looking
- MOM WHERE ARE YOU

Their brain is trying to process seven different social universes simultaneously while also really wanting that swing. No wonder someone ends up crying. Usually the mom.

The Friend Universe Paradox

"Why can't you play nicely with friends?"

Because "friend" means different things at different ages:

AGE 3: "Friend" = **Any child currently near me who hasn't taken my stuff** (yet)

AGE 4: "Friend" = **Child who has toy I want**

AGE 5: "Friend" = **Child who plays what I want to play**

AGE 6: "Friend" = **Child I play with sometimes when forced**

AGE 7: "Friend" = **Child I choose to be with** (revolutionary concept)

AGE 8: "Friend" = **Child who likes what I like**

AGE 9: "Friend" = **Complex reciprocal relationship**

AGE 30: "Friend" = **Person I see twice a year and text memes to**

When a four-year-old says "He's not my friend anymore!" about someone they've played with for years, they mean "He won't give me the truck right now." The relationship universe doesn't exist yet—only the immediate interaction universe.

Friendship, to them, resets every time someone takes a nap.

The Sharing Spiral

Let's map what "sharing" actually requires:

1. **Object awareness:** This thing exists
2. **Possession understanding:** I have it
3. **Other awareness:** They exist separately from me (shocking discovery)
4. **Desire recognition:** They want it
5. **Empathy activation:** Their want matters (why though?)
6. **Future projection:** I'll get it back (lying adults)
7. **Impulse override:** Don't grab it back
8. **Social reward understanding:** Sharing gets praise (insufficient payment)
9. **Relationship building:** This maintains friendship (what friendship?)
10. **Reciprocity expectation:** They'll share with me later (they won't)

Ten complex operations for one "simple" act. And that's assuming the object survives the sharing, which with siblings, it won't.

Try This: The Sharing Ladder

Instead of "Share your toys," build the ladder:

LEVEL 1: *"Tommy wants the car too"*

LEVEL 2: *"Tommy feels sad without a car"*

LEVEL 3: *"You can give Tommy one car"*

LEVEL 4: *"You'll still have three cars"*

LEVEL 5: *"Tommy will be happy"*

LEVEL 6: *"Then you can play cars together"*

LEVEL 7: *"Unless Tommy drives his car wrong
then you take it back"*

Wait, scratch that last one.

You're building the social universe step by step, not assuming it exists. Each step is a small miracle of social understanding that adults take for granted.

The Sibling Social Disaster

Siblings operate in a different social universe than friends:

Friends:

- Choose to be together
- Can leave when upset
- Limited exposure
- Best behavior motivation
- Adult supervision usual
- Novel interaction value
- Go home eventually thank God

Siblings:

- Forced proximity
- Can't escape
- Constant exposure
- No performance motivation
- Often unsupervised
- Familiarity breeds contempt
- They LIVE here
- They're ALWAYS here
- Make them stop EXISTING

When parents say "Treat your sister like a friend," they're asking for universe translation that's nearly impossible. It's like asking someone to treat their cellmate like a houseguest. "Would you like some tea, person I'm forced to share existence with who saw me eat that booger yesterday?"

The Birthday Party Breakdown

Birthday parties are social universe explosions waiting to happen:

Birthday child universe:

- I'm special today
- Everything is mine
- Everyone came for me
- I get all the attention
- My rules apply
- These are MY presents
- Why is anyone else even talking?
- This is basically my coronation

Guest universe:

- Party means fun for me
- Cake and games expected
- Present giving is confusing (I give away something?)
- Why is birthday child boss?
- When is it my turn to be special?
- Can I open the presents?
- I want to blow out candles
- This cake better not have nuts

These universes collide spectacularly when the birthday child won't share their new toys or let others blow out candles. They're not being selfish—they're operating in incompatible universes. It's like Mac vs PC but with more crying and cake.

The Apology Economy

"Say sorry to your friend."

But child social universe doesn't include:

- Genuine remorse (requires developed empathy)
- Relationship repair (requires continuity understanding)
- Social contracts (requires abstract thinking)
- Face-saving rituals (requires cultural knowledge)
- The complex dance of forgiveness
- Understanding that trust exists
- Knowing trust can break
- Caring that trust broke

So they say "SORRY!" and immediately repeat the offense. They've completed the required sound. The social universe that gives it meaning doesn't exist yet. It's like typing a password without understanding what login means.

The Fairness Fiction

"That's not fair!" might be the most common playground complaint. But fairness requires:

- Mathematical comparison
- Objective measurement
- Considering context
- Understanding equity vs. equality
- Recognizing different needs
- Accepting compromise
- Understanding that life isn't fair
- Accepting that sometimes you get less
- (Never accepting that sometimes you get less)

A four-year-old's "fair" means: "I don't like this outcome."
The complex social universe of justice doesn't exist. Only the
immediate universe of want/don't want.

> *"She got more!"*
> *"You had more yesterday."*
> *"THAT WAS YESTERDAY!"*

Yesterday's fairness doesn't carry over. Each day is a new fairness
audit. The universe resets at bedtime.

The Group Dynamics Disaster

Put three five-year-olds together:

> **Two children:** Parallel play possible, minimal conflict
> **Three children:** Alliance formation, exclusion, drama,
> someone's crying
> **Four children:** *Lord of the Flies*

Why? Because social universes multiply exponentially:

- **2 kids** = 2 relationships to manage
- **3 kids** = 6 relationships
- **4 kids** = 12 relationships
- **5 kids** = Complete social collapse

Their social processing maxes out at about 2-3 relationships. Add
more and universe collapse is guaranteed.

Try This: The Social Script

Give explicit social scripts for common situations:

"When someone has a toy you want, say:
'Can I have a turn when you're done?'"

"When you're done, say: 'Here, your turn!'"

"If they won't share, say: 'I'll find something else' and walk away"

"Don't say: 'I'm telling!' That's social suicide"

You're providing social universe navigation tools they can't create yet. It's like giving them a GPS for playground politics.

The Tattling Translation

"He's not following the rules!"

Tattling isn't snitching. It's social universe construction. They're trying to understand:

- Rules exist
- Rules should be followed
- But he's not following them
- This breaks my understanding
- Adult needs to fix this
- Universe must be restored
- WHY ISN'T ANYONE FIXING THIS

When we dismiss tattling, we're dismissing their attempt to understand social order. Better to acknowledge: "You're right, that's the rule. But sometimes people make mistakes. Like when you ate that cookie before dinner."

"That was different!" It's always different when it's them.

The Competitive Universe

"I won! I won! I'm the best! You're all losers! I'm amazing! Look at me! I WON!"

(Two minutes later)

"I HATE this game! It's STUPID! The game is BROKEN! You CHEATED! I'M NEVER PLAYING AGAIN!"

Same child, same game, different outcome. Competition requires holding multiple universes:

- Rules universe
- Performance universe
- Comparison universe
- Emotional regulation universe
- Future attempt universe
- Grace in victory universe (nonexistent)
- Grace in defeat universe (super nonexistent)

When they lose, all universes collapse to: "This is bad and wrong and I hate everything." They're not poor sports. They're experiencing total universe failure. Their entire understanding of existence is being challenged by a game of Candy Land.

The Inclusion Illusion

"Include everyone!"

But inclusion requires understanding:

- Others have feelings
- Others want to belong
- My fun isn't the only fun
- Games can accommodate different skills

- Friendship isn't finite
- Being kind costs nothing
- Actually it costs a lot when you're five
- Everything is zero-sum when you're five

When a child refuses to include someone, they're not mean. They're protecting their limited social resources. Adding another person might break their carefully balanced play universe. It's like asking someone to add another player to their chess game mid-match.

The Bathroom Exclusion Society

Nothing reveals social universe complexity like elementary school bathroom dynamics:

"Can I come to the bathroom with you?"
"We're best friends now!"
(Literally just about bathroom company)

The social currency of bathroom accompaniment is complex:

- Who asks who
- Who says yes
- Who else is included
- Who's excluded
- The politics of hand washing
- The power of paper towel distribution

Adults think kids waste time in bathrooms. Kids are conducting complex social negotiations that determine playground hierarchy. The UN could learn from elementary bathroom politics.

What This Means

The social universe is the most complex universe children build. Every interaction requires navigating multiple relationships, unspoken rules, invisible expectations, and constantly shifting dynamics.

When a child fails socially, they're not mean or selfish or badly raised. They're attempting universe navigation with incomplete maps, broken compasses, and no GPS. While blindfolded. On a unicycle.

Understanding this changes how we respond:
- We provide explicit social scripts
- We build one social skill at a time
- We acknowledge the complexity
- We celebrate small successes

The child who can't "just be nice"? They're trying to navigate New York City social dynamics with a map of Cleveland. In crayon. That they drew themselves. While someone keeps changing the streets.

Help them draw better maps. One playdate at a time. One meltdown at a time. One "that's not fair!" at a time.

And remember: even adults don't really understand sharing. We just got better at pretending we're okay with it.

CHAPTER 10

The Midnight Water Phenomenon

It's 2 AM.

"Mommy, I need water."

You stumble to the kitchen, fill a cup, bring it to their room.

"NOOOO! Not THAT cup! The BLUE cup!"

You're exhausted. They're melting down. Over a cup.

At 2 AM. You're googling *'Can children be legally declared nocturnal?'* (Apparently not. You checked.)

But here's what's really happening: When children are tired, stressed, hungry, or overwhelmed, their fragile word universes don't just weaken—they fragment into pieces, and each piece becomes desperately important. The blue cup isn't just a preference. It's the last functioning piece of their universe, and if that goes wrong, everything goes wrong.

The Collapse Sequence

Universe collapse follows a predictable pattern, like a very annoying weather system:

Stage 1: Fraying (tired but functional)

- Words still work but take longer to process
- Can follow single instructions
- Emotional universes wobbling but standing
- Might put shoes on wrong feet
- Still basically human

Stage 2: Fragmenting (approaching breakdown)

- Abstract words lose meaning first
- Only concrete, immediate words work
- Emotional regulation going offline
- Definitely shoes on wrong feet
- Possibly wearing shoes on hands

Stage 3: Collapse (full meltdown territory)

- Only sensory/physical words remain
- Everything becomes hyper-specific
- No flexibility, no substitutions
- Single universe focus
- THE BLUE CUP OR ELSE

Stage 4: Shutdown (beyond meltdown)

- No words work
- Pure sensory experience
- Fight/flight/freeze only
- Might be under furniture
- Communicating in screams
- Parent considering witness protection

The blue cup meltdown? That's Stage 3. "Water" has fragmented into:

- The specific blue cup (visual universe)
- The cold but not too cold (temperature universe)
- The amount that looks right (spatial universe)
- The way mom holds it (social universe)
- The three sips ritual (sequence universe)
- No ice because ice is scary at night (logic left the building)

Change any element and it's not "water" anymore. It's something else, something wrong, something that makes an exhausted brain work harder when it has nothing left to give.

The Hunger Collapse

"What do you want for lunch?"
"I DON'T KNOW!" (crying)

"How about a sandwich?"
"NOOOOO!"

"Soup?"
"I HATE SOUP!"

"What DO you want?"
"I DON'T KNOOOOOW!"
(Both crying now)

They're not being difficult. When blood sugar drops, the brain triages:

First to go: Abstract thinking
Then: Decision-making
Then: Language processing
Then: Emotional regulation
Finally: Basic motor skills
Last remaining: Pure rage at existence

Asking a hungry child to choose between options is like asking someone drowning to pick a swimming stroke. The choosing universe is offline. They need food first, decisions later.

Try This: The Rescue Meal

Keep a "rescue meal" that requires zero decisions:

- Always the same thing (crackers and cheese)
- Always available
- No choices needed
- Quick to prepare
- Boring enough they won't request it when not desperate

"You're too hungry to choose. Here's your rescue snack. We'll talk about lunch after."

You're not giving in. You're recognizing biological universe collapse and responding appropriately. It's triage, not surrender.

The Transition Collapse

Why do children melt down:

- Leaving the park
- Getting out of the bath
- Turning off screens

- Going to bed
- Coming inside
- Leaving anywhere fun
- Arriving anywhere not fun
- Existing in general

Transitions require shifting between entire universes. The park universe has different physics than the car universe. The bath universe has different rules than the pajama universe.

Adults shift universes constantly, unconsciously. Like changing channels. But for children, each transition is like being asked to switch languages mid-sentence while also changing clothes and forgetting everything they knew. The effort required can trigger instant collapse.

The Stages of Transition Grief

Watch the predictable stages:

1. **Announcement:** *"Five more minutes"*
   - (Universe shift warning)
   - Child ignores, hopes you'll forget

2. **Resistance:** *"NOOO! Ten more minutes!"*
   - (Brain protecting current universe)
   - Negotiation attempt

3. **Bargaining:** *"Two more minutes? One more?"*
   - (Trying to delay shift)
   - Getting desperate

4. **Anger: "*I HATE YOU! This is STUPID!*"**
   - (Universe shift failing)
   - Emotional regulation gone

5. **Collapse: Complete meltdown**
   - (Universe shift failure)
   - Now being carried to car

6. **Acceptance: Asleep in car seat**
   - (Universe finally shifted)

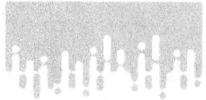

The Sunday Night Phenomenon

Sunday night before Monday school. Every week. Same meltdown. Same universe collision.

It's not about school (usually). It's about universe overwhelm. Their brain is trying to simultaneously:

- Let go of weekend universe (fun, relaxed, late bedtime)
- Anticipate school universe (structure, early, performance)
- Process transition anxiety (change is scary)
- Manage time concept stress (tomorrow is both forever and too soon)
- Hold multiple tomorrow scenarios (what if bad things?)
- Remember they didn't do that homework
- Realize they lost their library book
- Wonder if their friend still likes them
- Panic about everything

That's eight universes colliding. No wonder they can't sleep, everything is wrong, their socks feel weird.

The Birthday Party Collapse

Birthday parties are universe collision events designed to create meltdowns:

- **Excitement universe** (fun!)
- **Social universe** (so many kids!)
- **Sensory universe** (noise! lights! sugar!)
- **Routine universe** (broken!)
- **Expectation universe** (presents!)
- **Performance universe** (everyone watching!)
- **Competition universe** (games!)
- **Sugar crash universe** (inevitable!)

Watch a four-year-old at their own party:

- **Hour 1:** Ecstatic
- **Hour 2:** Hyper
- **Hour 3:** Crying over nothing
- **Hour 4:** Complete meltdown
- **Hour 5:** Passed out in pile of wrapping paper

They're not being ungrateful. They're experiencing universe overload. Every good thing becomes too much when universes collide. It's like trying to watch five movies simultaneously while eating cake and being hugged by everyone you know.

The Holiday Hangover

Christmas morning: Joy! Presents! Magic! Christmas afternoon: Crying because the box is more interesting than the toy. Christmas evening: Full meltdown because sister breathed near them December 26th: Child ???

The holiday universe collision creates a special kind of chaos:

- **Routine:** Destroyed
- **Expectations:** Sky high
- **Reality:** Can't match expectations
- **Sugar consumption:** Lethal levels
- **Sleep schedule:** What sleep schedule?
- **Relatives:** Everywhere
- **Sensory input:** Maximum
- **Parents:** Also melting down

The post-holiday meltdown isn't ingratitude. It's universe collapse from overstimulation. They literally can't process any more joy. The happiness tank is full and overflowing and now everything is wet and sticky.

The Recovery Patterns

Different children recover from universe collapse differently:

The Sleepers: Need to shut down completely, reset through sleep
- Just put them to bed
- Even at 4 PM
- Even in public
- Sleep is universe repair

The Movers: Need physical activity to rebuild universes
- Run laps around house
- Jump on trampoline
- Dance party
- Movement is universe rebuilding

The Hiders: Need quiet, dark spaces to reconstruct
- Under bed
- In closet
- Behind couch
- Darkness is universe restoration

The Clingers: Need physical contact to borrow your stable universes
- Must be touching you
- Possibly inside your shirt
- Becomes additional limb
- Contact is universe sharing

The Talkers: Need to verbally process the collapse
- Won't stop talking
- Repeating same story
- Making no sense
- Words are universe reconstruction

The Sorters: Need to organize something to rebuild order
- Lining up toys
- Sorting by color
- Arranging and rearranging
- Order is universe repair

Knowing your child's recovery pattern changes everything. Stop trying to talk a Hider out of the closet. Stop trying to calm a Mover who needs to run. They're not avoiding recovery—they're pursuing it in the way their brain requires.

The Proactive Prevention

Once you understand universe collapse, you can prevent it:

Morning Protection:
- Wake them 10 minutes earlier than needed
- No decisions for first 20 minutes
- Same breakfast routine
- Clothes laid out night before
- No surprises
- No rushing
- Accept that mornings take forever

Transition Bridges:
- Visual timers for universe shift warning
- Transition objects (bring a toy from home to car)
- Narrative bridges ("When we get home, we'll...")
- Sensory preparation ("It will be loud at the store")

Energy Monitoring:
- Universe capacity decreases as day progresses
- Complex activities early, simple later
- No new learning after 6 PM

- Protect the hour before bed
- Lower all expectations after 7 PM

The Sibling Collision

When one child's universe collapses, it triggers a chain reaction:

Child A: Melting down about cup
Child B: Upset by the noise
Child C: Taking advantage of chaos
Dog: Hiding under bed (smart)

This is why one child's meltdown becomes whole family chaos. It's not bad parenting. It's universe collapse spreading like wildfire. Or like stomach flu but louder.

Try This: The Isolation Protocol

When you see universe collapse starting:

1. **Physically separate** (stop the contagion)
   - One child per room
   - Or one child per parent
   - Or one child to grandma's house

2. **Lower sensory input** (reduce the load)
   - Lights dimmer
   - Sounds quieter
   - Fewer demands
   - Stop talking

3. **Simplify to concrete** (no abstract concepts)
   - *"Sit here"*
   - *"Drink this"*
   - *"Hold teddy"*
   - Nothing complex

4. **Wait for Stage 1 recovery** before attempting repair
   - Could be 5 minutes
   - Could be 5 hours
   - Could be tomorrow

You're not giving in or letting them win. You're performing universe triage.

The Repair Window

After universe collapse, there's a critical window for learning:

Too soon: Still too fragmented to process
Too late: Event disconnected from feeling
Just right: About 20-30 minutes after calm returns

This is when you can:
- Name what happened
- Connect body feelings to emotions
- Build prevention strategies
- Practice universe-building
- Pretend you have everything under control

"Your universes got too tired to work. That's why the cup felt so important."

You're teaching them to recognize collapse before it happens. Eventually. Maybe by college.

What This Means

Universe collapse isn't defiance, manipulation, or bad behavior. It's neurological overwhelm. When we understand this:

- We stop taking it personally
- We respond with support, not punishment
- We prevent rather than react
- We teach recognition and recovery
- We accept that some days everyone melts down
- We keep emergency chocolate hidden for ourselves

The midnight water phenomenon isn't about water or cups or control. It's about a small brain trying to maintain universes that are dissolving. When we see it this way, our response changes from frustration to compassion.

And that changes everything—for them and for us.

Even if it means we're filling the blue cup at 2 AM while questioning all our life choices. Because tomorrow night it might be the red cup. Or the cup with the dolphins. Or no cup, water must be consumed directly from the faucet like a cat.

Parenting: It's a universe collapse adventure, and nobody gets out unscathed.

PART IV

The Words
That Break

CHAPTER 11

The Pronoun Problem

What if a three-year-old tried to navigate pronouns:

"You want cookie!" (meaning: I want a cookie)

"Me going to store with you?" (meaning: I'm going with you?)

"Give it to you!" (while reaching for something themselves)

"You do it!" (meaning: I'll do it)

What if this isn't confusion? What if this is a child attempting to navigate the most complex linguistic concept humans have invented: perspective-dependent meaning.

Think about how insane pronouns are:
- *"I"* means whoever is speaking
- *"You"* means whoever is listening
- These switch constantly
- *"Me"* and *"you"* can refer to the same person

depending on who's talking
- *"We"* might include you, or might not
- *"They"* could be anyone not here
- Sometimes *"you"* means everyone in general
- Royal *"we"* exists for some reason

Every pronoun is a shape-shifting universe that completely depends on who's speaking, who's listening, and who's being discussed. The same physical person can be "I," "you," "he," "him," "that kid," and "the one who ate all the crackers" all within the same thirty-second conversation.

It's linguistic chaos. And we expect three-year-olds to master it.

The Perspective Impossibility

To use pronouns correctly, a child needs to:
1. Understand they exist (around 18 months)
2. Understand others exist separately (around 2 years)
3. Understand perspectives can differ (around 3-4 years)
4. Track who's speaking right now (continuous)
5. Mentally rotate perspective (around 4-5 years)
6. Apply correct pronoun from that perspective (around 5-6 years)
7. Do this in real-time during conversation (around 6-7 years)
8. Not lose their mind (impossible)

That's eight cognitive operations happening simultaneously. When a three-year-old says "You want up!" while raising their arms, they're not confused. They're at step 2 of an 8-step process. Give them a break. And maybe a cookie. You want cookie. I mean, they want cookie. We all want cookies.

The Mirror Stage

Around age 2-3, children often go through what researchers call "pronoun reversal." They use "you" for themselves and "I" for others. This isn't random—it's logical.

Think about it: Every time someone talks to them, that person says "you" while meaning the child. Every time someone refers to themselves, they say "I." So the child learns:

- *"You"* = me (because that's what everyone calls me)
- *"I"* = other people (because that's what they call themselves)

It's perfectly logical. It's also completely wrong. And it takes years to untangle.

It's like everyone's been calling you "buddy" your whole life so you think that's your name, then finding out "buddy" means whoever someone's talking to. Mind. Blown.

The Conversation Whiplash

Watch this conversation between a parent and three-year-old:

Parent: "Do you want juice?"
Child: *"You want juice!"* (meaning yes, I want juice)
Parent: *"I don't want juice. Do YOU want juice?"*
Child: *"You don't want juice!"* (confused, still meaning themselves)
Parent: (frustrated) *"I'm asking if YOU want juice!"*
Child: (near tears) *"YOU WANT JUICE!"*
Parent: (gives up, pours juice)
Child: (happy)
Dog: (hoping for spilled juice)

Both people are being logical. Both are speaking different languages. The child is using "you" consistently to mean themselves. The parent is using pronouns correctly. Neither can understand why the other is being so difficult.

The Name Solution

This is why children often refer to themselves by name well into preschool:

> *"Sarah hungry!"*
> *"Sarah go park?"*
> *"Give Sarah cookie!"*
> *"Sarah's toy!"*
> *"No touch Sarah!"*
> *"Sarah do it MYSELF!"*

Names are stable. "Sarah" always means Sarah, no matter who's talking. It's the linguistic equivalent of solid ground in a world of shifting perspectives.

Parents often worry about third-person speech. "Why won't they say 'I'?" But the child has found a brilliant solution to an impossible problem. They've opted out of the pronoun universe entirely. It's like refusing to play a game where the rules keep changing.

Try This: The Pronoun Bridge

Instead of correcting, build bridges:

> **Child:** *"Sarah wants cookie."*
> **Parent:** *"Oh, Sarah wants a cookie? I hear that Sarah wants a cookie. You want a cookie!"*

You're showing them the translation without demanding they use it. Each time, you're building the connection between their stable name-universe and the shifting pronoun-universe.

Don't say: "Say 'I want a cookie'" They'll just repeat: "I want a cookie" (meaning you want a cookie) Now everyone's confused and nobody has cookies.

The Invisible Speakers Problem

"They said we can't go."

Who's "they"? The child has no idea. "They" is anyone not currently visible. Could be:

- Teachers
- Parents
- Kids at school
- The government
- Imaginary friends
- The dogs next door
- The voices in the walls
- Whoever makes rules

Without theory of mind fully developed, "they" becomes a mysterious authority that exists somewhere outside the current room. This is why children will confidently report that "they said" something completely made up. In their universe, "they" is just "not here"—and not-here people could have said anything.

"They said I can have ice cream for dinner."
"Who's they?"
"They!"
"Where are they?"
"Not here."
Checkmate.

The "We" Confusion

"We" might be the most complex pronoun of all:

- Inclusive we (you and me)
- Exclusive we (me and others, not you)
- Royal we (just me being formal)
- Collective we (our whole group/family/species)
- Editorial we (what newspapers use)
- Parental we (we need to use the potty = you need to use the potty)

What if a four-year-old hasn't subdivided "we" yet. When you say "We need to clean up," they might:

- Wait for you to start (inclusive we)
- Look for siblings (family we)
- Think you mean yourself (royal we)
- Stand there confused (we overload)
- Start cleaning (miraculous understanding) The last one never happens.

?

The Question Reversal

"What's your name?"
"Your name!"
"No, what's YOUR name?"
"YOUR NAME!"
(Everyone frustrated)

The child isn't being silly. They're answering exactly what they heard. In their experience:

- When people talk to them, *"your"* means the child
- So *"your name"* means their own name
- They're trying to tell you their name by saying *"your"*

It's like everything is backwards in a mirror. They're seeing the reflection, not the reality. They're technically correct from their perspective, which is the most frustrating kind of correct.

The Possession Puzzle

"Mine" and "yours" add another layer of complexity:

"This is mine!" (whoever is speaking owns it)
"That's yours!" (whoever is listening owns it)
"It's theirs!" (someone else entirely owns it)
"It's ours!" (maybe we share it?)
"It's nobody's!" (philosophical crisis at around age 4)

But ownership itself is a universe still under construction. What if a three-year-old says "MINE!" about everything, they're not selfish.

They're testing the boundaries of a concept that requires:

- Understanding ownership exists
- Knowing ownership can transfer
- Tracking who currently possesses what
- Using the right pronoun from the right perspective
- Accepting that not everything is theirs
- (Never actually accepting this)

That's why "share yours" is incomprehensible. "Yours" means mine when you say it to me, but mine is mine, so share mine? But it's mine? The circular logic breaks their brain.

The Storytelling Disaster

Listen to a four-year-old tell a story:

"And then he said—no wait, she said—and then they went—who went?—I went—no, you were there—no wait, he was there—who's he?—the guy—which guy?—you know, him!"

They're not confused about what happened. They're drowning in perspective shifts. Every character requires changing the entire pronoun universe. It's like trying to tell a story while constantly switching languages, except the languages are all English but the words mean different things each time.

By the end, nobody knows who did what, everyone's confused, and the child is frustrated that you don't understand their perfectly clear story about how "he took the thing from her and gave it to them but they didn't want it so you had it but I wanted it."

The Social Catastrophe

Pronouns gone wrong create social disasters:

Child (pointing at larger person): *"Why is he fat?"*
Parent: *"Shhhh!"*
Child (louder): *"WHY IS HE FAT?"*
Parent: (dying inside)
Large person: (heard everything)
Universe: (collapsed)

The child doesn't understand that "he" connects to a real person who can hear them. In their universe:

- *"He"* is just a label for that person over there
- That person and *"he"* aren't connected in awareness
- Speaking about *"he"* is different from speaking TO him
- Volume is irrelevant to *"he"* status

The social universe where pronouns carry relationships and using them incorrectly causes offense hasn't formed yet. They might as well be saying "Why is blue-shirt tall?" It's just descriptor words to them.

The Gender Pronoun Problem

Now add gender to the confusion:

"Is that a he or a she?"
"That's a person."
"But he or she?"

"Why does it matter?"
"I need to know for my sentence!"

Children are trying to figure out that:

- Some people are "he"
- Some people are "she"
- Some people are "they"
- You can't always tell by looking
- Getting it wrong upsets people
- But everyone looks the same to a three-year-old
- Except some have long hair but that's not reliable
- This is exhausting

They're not being rude when they get pronouns wrong. They can barely handle "I" and "you"—adding gender selection is like asking them to solve calculus while juggling.

Building Pronoun Universes

Instead of constant correction, build systematically:

STAGE 1: Stable Self
"Yes, Sarah wants cookie. Sarah is hungry."

STAGE 2: Introduction Bridge
"Sarah wants cookie. You want a cookie!"

STAGE 3: Parallel Tracks
"You want a cookie and I'll have water."

STAGE 4: Perspective Practice
"Tell daddy: 'I want a cookie.'"
(They'll probably say: *"You want a cookie, daddy!"*)

STAGE 5: Complex Perspectives
"What do you think he wants?"
(Brain explosion)

Each stage builds on the last. Skipping stages creates confusion. It's like teaching someone to run before they can walk, except they also have to run backwards while explaining why they're running.

The Pronoun Game

Make it a game:

"Let's play the switching game!"
"When I point to you, you say 'me!'"
"When you point to me, I say 'me!'"
"When I point to myself, I say 'me!'"
"When you point to yourself, you say 'me!'"

Watch their face as they realize "me" moves around. It's like watching someone discover gravity exists. Mind-blowing and slightly concerning.

What This Means

The pronoun problem isn't a problem—it's a window into the incredible cognitive feat children are attempting. They're not just learning words. They're learning that:

- Perspectives exist
- Perspectives differ

- Language shifts with perspective
- They need to track all perspectives simultaneously
- And translate in real-time
- While also remembering what they wanted
- Which was probably a cookie

When a child says "You want up!" with raised arms, they're not wrong. They're showing you exactly where they are in building one of the most complex universes humans navigate.

They're doing remarkably well for someone who recently discovered they're not actually part of your body. The fact that they can communicate at all is miraculous.

So maybe when they say "You want cookie," just give them the cookie. You both know what they mean. The pronouns will sort themselves out eventually. Probably by kindergarten. Maybe by college. Definitely by their own parenthood when they hear their child say "You want up!" and suddenly understand the beautiful confusion of it all.

CHAPTER 12

The "Don't" Processing Problem

Here's something that will change how you give instructions forever: Children's brains have a difficult time processing *"don't"* without first processing the thing you're telling them *not* to do.

> *"Don't run!"* Their brain processes: **RUN!** (don't)
>
> *"Don't touch that!"* Their brain: **TOUCH THAT!** (don't)
>
> *"Don't spill your juice!"* Their brain: **SPILL!** (don't)
>
> *"Don't wake the baby!"* Their brain: **WAKE BABY!** (don't)
>
> Baby: (now awake) **You:** (now crying)

The action word lights up their motor cortex before the negation can catch up. It's like their brain is a YouTube video and "don't" is trying to load on slow WiFi. By the time "don't" buffers, they're already running. With your juice. Toward the baby.

The Neurological Sequence

Here's what happens in the split second after you say "Don't run":

Around **0-50ms**: Sound waves hit ear

Around **50-100ms**: Auditory cortex decodes sounds into words

Around **100-150ms**: "Run" activates motor cortex
(body prepares to run)

Around **150- 200ms**: Prefrontal cortex receives "don't"

Around **200-250ms**: Attempt to inhibit motor response

Around **250-300ms**: Success or failure of inhibition

Around **301ms**: Child is running

Around **302ms**: You're yelling louder

In adults, this happens so fast we don't notice. But in children under 7, that inhibition step (around 200-250ms) often fails. The motor cortex is fully developed. The prefrontal cortex that handles "don't"? Still under construction for another 20 years.

It's like having a Ferrari engine with bicycle brakes. And the bicycle brakes are made of cheese. And the cheese is melting.

The Positive Instruction Revolution

Instead of fighting neurology, work with it:

Don't → Do:
- "Don't run" → "Walk slowly"
- "Don't yell" → "Use your quiet voice"
- "Don't hit" → "Gentle touches"
- "Don't throw" → "Keep it in your hands"
- "Don't jump" → "Feet on floor"
- "Don't spill" → "Hold with two hands"
- "Don't draw on walls" → "Paper only"
- "Don't eat the Play-Doh" → Actually, maybe just hide the Play-Doh

You're not just avoiding tantrums. You're speaking directly to the part of their brain that's actually online.

Try This: The Don't Diary

Keep track for one day of every "don't" instruction you give. Mark whether child:

- Immediately did the thing you said don't do
- Paused, looked confused, then did it
- Successfully stopped themselves
- Did something else problematic instead
- Looked at you with malicious compliance and did it slowly

Most parents discover they say "don't" 50+ times a day, with less than 20% success rate. The other 80%? They're fighting their child's neurology. It's like arm wrestling with physics. Physics always wins.

The Image Problem

"Don't think about pink elephants."

What happened? You thought about pink elephants. Your brain had to create the image before it could negate it.

Same with kids, but worse. When you say "Don't spill," their brain creates:

- Visual image of spilling
- Motor memory of spilling motion
- Sensory prediction of liquid falling
- Maybe a memory of last time they spilled
- The satisfaction of watching liquid flow

They've mentally rehearsed spilling before the "don't" arrives. No wonder it happens so often. You're basically giving them a spilling tutorial with a weak "please don't" at the end.

The Don't Spiral

Watch how "don't" instructions escalate:

Parent: *"Don't touch that"*
Child: (touches it)

Parent: *"I said DON'T touch!"*
Child: (touches it again, maintaining eye contact)

Parent: *"DON'T! TOUCH! THAT!"*
Child: (touching intensifies)

Parent: *"WHY ARE YOU STILL TOUCHING IT?"*
Child: "You keep talking about touching!"

The child has a point. Every "don't touch" is reinforcing "TOUCH" in their motor cortex. It's like saying "Don't think about cookies" forty times and wondering why someone wants cookies.

Cultural Brain Differences

Some languages handle negation differently, and it shows in behavior:

English: Negation comes first *("Don't touch")*
- Kids hear action word most clearly
- Higher rates of doing prohibited thing

German: Negation sometimes comes at end (*"Fass das nicht an"*)
- Action still processed first
- Similar challenges

Japanese: Different negation structures entirely
- Some studies suggest easier prohibition learning
- Maybe relates to linguistic structure

The way your language structures negation literally affects how your child might process prohibition. English is basically set up to make kids do exactly what you tell them not to do. Thanks, English.

The Stress Multiplication Effect

When a child is stressed, tired, or hungry, "don't" processing gets worse:

Normal state: 30% failure rate
Tired: 60% failure rate
Hungry: 70% failure rate
Overstimulated: 80% failure rate
Meltdown mode: 95% failure rate
Birthday party sugar crash: 100% failure rate
December 26th: Don't even try

The more they need to stop, the less able they are to process "don't." It's cruelly ironic—the times we most need "don't" to work are when it's most likely to fail.

The Alternative Actions Framework

Children's brains need somewhere to GO, not just somewhere to STOP. Empty space is terrifying to a young brain.

Instead of stopping action, redirect it:

"Don't touch the stove" becomes:

- *"Hands on counter while I cook"*
- *"Stand by this chair"*
- *"Hold this spoon for me"*
- *"Be my taste tester over here"*

You're giving their motor cortex a job instead of asking it to shut down. It's like redirecting a river instead of trying to dam it. With your bare hands. While the river is made of hyperactive four-year-olds.

Try This: The Replacement Game

Practice with your child when calm:

"When I say *'don't run,'* you say *'walk slowly!'"*
"When I say *'don't yell,'* you say *'quiet voice!'"*
"When I say *'don't hit,'* you say *'gentle touches!'*"

Make it a game. They're teaching their brain the translations. Eventually, they'll auto-correct internally. Maybe. Hopefully. By high school.

The Emergency Override

"But what about danger? Sometimes I need them to STOP!"

For true emergencies, skip "don't" entirely:

"STOP!" (full stop, no action word)

"FREEZE!" (positive action that means stillness)

"STATUE!" (fun version that means stop)

"BANANA!" (whatever word you've practiced)

These work because they're positive commands for stillness, not negated commands for action.

Practice these when not in danger:

- Play freeze dance
- Play statue game
- Practice emergency stops
- Explain that "BANANA" is your family's secret stop word
- Watch them yell "BANANA" at inappropriate times

Build the neural pathway when calm so it's available in crisis. Like a fire drill, but for not running into traffic.

The Developmental Timeline

Around age 2-3: *"Don't"* is meaningless noise
- Only hear action words
- No inhibition capacity
- Need physical intervention
- Will definitely do the thing

Around age 4-5: *"Don't"* sometimes works
- 30% success rate
- Better when calm
- Still need positive alternatives
- Eye contact while doing the thing

Around age 6-7: *"Don't"* becoming functional
- 50% success rate
- Can sometimes self-correct
- Still process action first
- Delayed compliance possible

Around age 8-10: *"Don't"* mostly reliable
- 70% success rate
- Can inhibit most impulses
- Still struggle when stressed
- Roll eyes but comply

Around age 11-13: *"Don't"* works but they're choosing not to
- Brain can process it
- Rebellion is different issue
- Good luck with that

Around age 25: Prefrontal cortex fully developed
- *"Don't"* fully functional
- (Yes, 25. Not a typo.)
- (Your brain isn't done until 25)
- (Explains a lot about your twenties)

The Sibling Domino Effect

"Don't hit your sister!"

What the hitter hears: **HIT SISTER** (don't)
What the sister hears: **HIT? SOMEONE'S HITTING?**
What the baby hears: **LOUD VOICES DANGER**
What the dog hears: **EXCITEMENT! CHAOS! ZOOMIES TIME!**

One "don't" instruction just activated:

- One hitting motion
- One defensive response
- One startle response
- One case of dog zoomies

The hitter's motor cortex is primed for hitting. The sister is now hypervigilant for attacks. The baby is scared. The dog is running in circles. You've created chaos trying to prevent it.

Alternative:

"Hands to yourself. Sister, come here."

Calm. Directed. No activation of violence concepts. Dog remains calm. (Dog never remains calm.)

The Don't Loop of Doom

Sometimes we get stuck in don't loops:

"Don't whine" (Child whines about being told not to whine)
"I said don't whine!" (Whining intensifies)
"Stop whining!" (Now crying)
"Don't cry!" (Sobbing)
"DON'T SOB!" (Existential crisis for everyone)

Each "don't" is creating the thing you're trying to stop. It's like putting out a fire with gasoline. While the fire is your child's emotional regulation. And the gasoline is your frustration.

The Positive Household Experiment

Try this: a week of no "don't" instructions. The rules:

1. Only positive instructions allowed
2. Had to say what TO do, not what NOT to do
3. Everyone participated (kids could call out parent "don'ts")
4. Penalty jar for "don'ts" (money could go to ice cream fund)

Results to look for:

Day 1: Exhausting, caught themselves 100+ times, owed $47 to ice cream fund

Day 3: Getting easier, kids responding better

Day 5: Natural rhythm emerging

Day 7: 70% reduction in conflicts

Week 2: Forgot they were doing experiment, still worked

Ice cream fund: Achieved annual budget funding

The kids weren't better behaved. The instructions were better aligned with their neurology.

The Creative Alternatives

Sometimes you need to get creative.

Instead of "Don't wake the baby":

- *"Ninja mode activated"*
- *"Quiet as mice"*
- *"Sleeping baby challenge"*

Instead of "Don't touch":

- *"Hands behind back"*
- *"Look with eyes only"*
- *"Museum hands"* (clasped behind)

Instead of "Don't interrupt":

- *"Wait for the pause"*
- *"Hold that thought"*
- *"Put your words in your pocket"*

You're giving them something TO do with the energy that wants to do the don't thing.

What This Means

Using "don't" with young children is like typing with autocorrect that changes every word to its opposite. You type "don't run" and it autocorrects to "RUN FASTER!" You're fighting their brain's programming.

This isn't permissive parenting. It's neurologically-informed parenting. You're not lowering standards—you're raising communication effectiveness.

When you understand the "don't" processing problem:

- Instructions become clearer
- Compliance increases
- Frustration decreases
- Children feel more successful
- You stop fighting physics
- The dog stays calmer (unlikely)

They're not defying you when they do what you said "don't" do. What if their brain literally heard "do" louder than "don't?"

So tomorrow, when you catch yourself saying "Don't—" stop. Breathe. Think: What DO I want them to do? Then say that instead.

> *"Don't run!"* becomes *"Walking feet!"*
> *"Don't yell!"* becomes *"Inside voice!"*
> *"Don't hit!"* becomes *"Gentle touches!"*

And maybe, just maybe, they'll actually do it.

Or they won't, but at least you'll know it's not because their brain autocorrected your instruction to its opposite. Small victories in parenting. We take what we can get.

CHAPTER 13

The Preposition Predicament

"Put your shoes BY the door."

Simple instruction, right? Let's unpack "by":

- Near but not touching?
- Touching but not on top?
- To the side but how far?
- On the floor next to it?
- On the shoe rack that's beside it?
- In the general vicinity?
- Within throwing distance?
- Same zip code?

Every preposition carries an entire spatial universe that we take for granted. But for a child, each preposition is a physics equation they can't solve. They're being asked to calculate spatial relationships with a brain that just recently figured out objects continue to exist when you can't see them.

No wonder the shoes end up in the refrigerator. At least they're "by" something.

The Spatial Universe Chaos

Adults have an internal GPS. Children have... optimistic guessing at best. Watch a four-year-old try to follow spatial instructions:

"Put the ball between the box and the wall." They might:

- Put it on top of the box (that's touching both, right?)
- Put it behind both
- Stand between the objects themselves, holding the ball
- Put it in the box (that's kind of between?)
- Throw it at the wall (near the box counts?)
- Give up and keep the ball
- Eat the ball (wait, what?)

They're not being difficult. They're trying to navigate three-dimensional spatial relationships with a brain that's still figuring out that up is opposite of down. Sometimes.

The On/In/Under Confusion

These seem basic. They're not:

ON:
- On the table (horizontal surface)
- On the wall (vertical surface???)
- On TV (inside the screen or physically on top?)
- On my mind (where exactly is that?)
- On time (time has a surface?)
- On fire (not literally on top of fire though)
- On purpose (purpose has location?)

IN:
- In the box (fully enclosed)
- In the yard (but it's outside?)
- In trouble (where is trouble located?)
- In a minute (time is a container?)
- In love (love has an interior?)
- In the mood (mood has space?)
- In your dreams (dreams have dimensions?)

UNDER:
- Under the bed (directly below)
- Under the weather (weather is above me?)
- Under pressure (pressure has weight?)
- Under consideration (considering is on top?)
- Underground (makes sense)
- Understand (standing under what exactly?)
- Underwear (wear under what? Under where?
  Dad joke achieved :)

Each preposition splits into physical and abstract universes that many children have difficulties reconciling. When you say "Put it on the table" then later say "You're on thin ice," they might literally check the floor for ice.

The Behind/In Front Nightmare

"Stand behind your sister."

Seems simple. But *"behind"* requires:
- Understanding she has a front and back
- Knowing which is which
- From whose perspective?
- What if she turns around?
- How far behind?
- Directly behind or generally behind?
- What if she backs up?
- Is behind her hair still behind?

Now she turns around. Are you still behind her? Or are you now in front? The child's brain explodes. Sister turns again. Now what? Sister spins in circles. The concept of "behind" ceases to exist. Everyone's dizzy. Mission failed.

Try This: The Position Game

Use yourself as the reference point first:

"Stand in front of ME" (clear, single perspective)
"Now beside ME" (still clear)
"Now behind ME" (you're not moving, easier to track)

Then gradually add complexity:

"Stand behind the chair" (object doesn't move)

"Stand behind the dog" (uh oh, it moves)

"Stand behind your sister" (she moves AND turns)

"Stand behind your shadow" (existential crisis)

Build spatial universe complexity gradually. Or watch your child stand in increasingly creative interpretations of "behind."

The Beside/Next To Crisis

"Sit beside your brother." But beside could mean:

- Directly sideways touching
- Nearby but not touching
- On the same furniture
- In the same general area
- To the right specifically
- To the left specifically
- Within punching distance
- Outside of punching distance (preferred)

The child sits across from brother.

"I said BESIDE!"

"I am beside! Beside the table!"

"BESIDE your BROTHER!"

"The table is beside my brother!"

They're confused. Across is beside from a different angle. Their spatial universe doesn't include fixed directional relationships yet. Everything is beside everything if you think about it wrong enough.

The Between Breakdown

"Between" might be the most complex preposition:

Physical between: Requires three reference points simultaneously

Temporal between: *"Between lunch and dinner"*
(when is that exactly?)

Abstract between: *"Between you and me"* (a secret space?)

Choosing between: "Between the red and blue" (they're not spatial)

Reading between the lines: (WHAT lines? WHERE?)

A four-year-old asked to stand "between" mom and dad might:

- Try to squeeze into non-existent space
- Stand in front of both
- Stand behind both
- Lay across both of them
- Give up and cry
- Become one with the floor

Three-point spatial calculation is graduate-level geometry for a preschool brain. It's like asking them to solve for X when they're still learning that X is a letter.

The Cultural Preposition Problem

Different cultures use space differently:

English: On the bus, in the car
German: Different prepositions entirely
Japanese: Spatial relationships include respect distances
Arabic: Right/left have religious significance
Finnish: 15 different cases that affect spatial meaning

Bilingual children aren't just learning two words—they're learning two completely different spatial universes. No wonder they mix them up. They're not confused, they're managing multiple incompatible physics systems in their head.

"Why did you put your shoes over the door?"
"You said over!"
"Over there, not literally over!"

The Above/Below Complexity

"The cup goes above the plate." Above requires:

- Vertical space understanding
- Gravity awareness
- Relative positioning
- Maintaining distance
- Not "on" but higher
- Higher but not too high
- Still reachable
- But elevated
- Physics degree helpful

The child puts the cup on the plate.
"No, ABOVE!"

They stack another plate on top.
"ABOVE not ON!"

They throw the cup at the ceiling.
"Not THAT above!"
Cup breaks. Everyone cries.

The Through/Around Impossibility

"Go through the door" vs "Go around the building"

Through requires understanding:
- Portals exist
- Objects have hollow spaces
- You can enter and exit
- The path penetrates
- Don't go through walls
- Unless it's a door
- Or a window (no wait)

Around requires:
- Objects have perimeters
- You can circle without touching
- The path avoids the object
- Multiple routes exist
- How far around?
- All the way around?
- Halfway around?

A three-year-old told to go "around" something might go over it, under it, or through it. They're all "not directly at it" which seems like the same thing. The dog goes under the fence, around the yard, and through the flowers. Dog understands prepositions perfectly. Dog chooses chaos.

Try This: The Preposition Path

Create an obstacle course using only preposition instructions:

"Go under the table"
"Around the chair"
"Through the doorway"
"Over the pillow"
"Between the toys"
"Behind the couch"
"Across the room"
"Into the kitchen"

Watch where confusion happens. Those are the prepositions that need work. Practice with body movement builds spatial universes faster than words. Plus everyone's tired afterward. Win-win.

The Invisible Distance Problem

"Stay near me" at the park.

Near is relative:
- Adult "near" = within eyesight (50 feet)
- Child "near" = touching or almost touching (2 feet)
- Teen "near" = same continent
- Dog "near" = can smell you (variable)

The child runs 20 feet away. You panic:
"I said stay NEAR!"
They: *"I AM near! I can see you!"*
You: *"That's not near!"*
They: *"It's nearer than China!"*

They have a point. The spatial universe for proximity hasn't calibrated to adult standards. "Near" is relative to your anxiety level, which they can't measure.

The Time-Space Confusion

English uses spatial prepositions for time:

- *"Before lunch"* (space word for time)
- *"After school"* (following in space?)
- *"During dinner"* (inside dinner?)
- *"Throughout the day"* (through space)
- *"Behind schedule"* (schedule has a back?)
- *"Ahead of time"* (time has a front?)
- *"In time"* (time is a container)
- *"On time"* (time has a surface)

Children who struggle with time concepts often struggle with prepositions first. They're the same universe expressing itself differently. When you say "We'll go after lunch," they might look behind their sandwich.

The Preposition Stack Attack

Sometimes we stack prepositions:

"Put it up on top of the shelf in the closet."

Child's brain:
- Up (which direction?)
- **On** (touching?)
- **Top** (highest point?)
- **Of** (possession?)
- **Shelf** (which one?)
- **In** (inside?)
- **Closet** (still processing shelf)

By the time they've processed all the prepositions, they've forgotten what "it" was. The item ends up on the floor. Mission failed successfully.

The Moving Reference Problem

"Put it in front of the TV."

But then you move the TV. Is the "front" space still there? Does front move with the TV? Is there a ghost front where the TV used to be? These are the questions that haunt three-year-olds.

> *"But I DID put it in front of the TV!"*
> *"The TV is over here now."*
> *"You said in front of the TV, not in front of where the TV is now!"*

Technically correct. The most frustrating kind of correct.

The Developmental Timeline

Around age 2-3: Only concrete touching prepositions
- **On** (means touching on top)
- **In** (means fully inside)
- **Up/down** (vertical movement only)
- **Everything else** is suggestions

Around age 3-4: Basic spatial relationships
- **Under, over** (still needs to touch)
- **Next to** (means very close)
- **Behind/front** (emerging)
- **Still putting** things in refrigerator

Around age 4-5: Complex spatial relationships
- **Between** (with difficulty)
- **Around** (sometimes)
- **Through** (getting there)
- Shoes **occasionally** near door

Around age 5-7: Abstract prepositions emerging
- **During, before, after**
- **Throughout, within**
- **Among, beside**
- Shoes **might** make it to door area

Around age 8+: Full preposition universe
- **All spatial relationships**
- **Abstract applications**
- **Metaphorical uses**
- **Still can't** find shoes

What This Means

When a child can't follow "simple" spatial instructions, they're not being careless. They're attempting complex geometric calculations without the neural architecture.

Every preposition is a universe of spatial relationships that takes years to map. When we understand this:

- We use gestures with prepositions
- We demonstrate rather than just describe
- We build from simple to complex
- We recognize the cognitive load
- We accept shoes will be everywhere

The child who puts their shoes in the wrong place? They're not defying you. They're navigating spatial universes with a compass they've never used before, no map, and a belief that "by" means "somewhere on Earth."

And honestly? Sometimes the shoes in the refrigerator is creative problem-solving. They're by the milk. The milk is by the door to the refrigerator. The refrigerator is by the kitchen door.

Technically, the shoes are by a door. Several degrees of separation, but still.

You can't argue with that logic. You can try, but you'll lose. The three-year-old has already moved on to putting socks in the toaster. They're by the bread. Don't ask.

CHAPTER 14

The Universe of "No"

Let's talk about the word children hear most and understand least: "No."

Watch a toddler's face when you say no. Sometimes they stop immediately. Sometimes they laugh and continue. Sometimes they melt down. Sometimes they pause, look at you, and do it anyway while maintaining eye contact.

We think they're testing us. They think we're making random sounds that sometimes correlate with facial expressions.

Here's what "no" means to an adult:
- Stop what you're doing
- That action is inappropriate/dangerous/not allowed
- This is a boundary
- I disapprove
- This rule applies now and in the future
- Consider the consequences

- This is categorically forbidden
- Learn from this for next time
- Possibly consider your life choices

Here's what "no" means to a two-year-old:
- Mom made the loud sound
- Her face is red
- Maybe pause?
- Resume activity
- Mom louder now

That's it. The entire moral, safety, and social universe we've packed into "no" doesn't exist yet.

The Category Problem

Adults organize "no" into invisible categories:

Safety Nos: Don't touch the stove (burns)
Social Nos: Don't yell in library (disturbs others)
Practical Nos: Don't pour juice on floor (makes mess)
Moral Nos: Don't hit people (causes harm)
Arbitrary Nos: Don't draw on walls (social convention
Parental Preference Nos: Don't touch my phone (it's mine)
Because I Said So Nos: Don't ask why (circular logic)

To a three-year-old, these are all identical: "times when adults make the no sound."

They might carefully avoid touching your phone (yesterday's big "no") while casually endangering their lives climbing furniture. They're not being deliberately defiant. The categories don't exist. Every "no" is a separate, unconnected event.

It's like having a list of random prohibitions:
- Don't wear purple on Tuesday
- Don't touch things that are 98.6 degrees
- Don't make sounds above 85 decibels in buildings with books
- Don't put liquid on horizontal surfaces at ground level

Without categories, it's just chaos.

The Now vs. Forever Problem

When you say "no," you mean:
- Don't do this now
- Don't do this later
- Don't do this tomorrow
- Don't do this ever
- Remember this rule
- Apply to similar situations
- Teach your future children this

When a toddler hears "no," they process:
- Stop current motion (maybe)
- For the next 3 seconds
- Unless you look away
- Then reset

That's why you have to say "no" to the same thing every single day. Sometimes every single hour. They're not forgetting. The concept that "no" extends through time doesn't exist yet. Each day is a new universe where the stove might be touchable.

"But we talked about this yesterday!"
"What's yesterday?"
Both valid points.

The Intensity Paradox

Parents escalate "no" intensity thinking it will help:

- *"No"* (ignored)
- *"No!"* (glance)
- *"NO!"* (pause)
- *"I said NO!"* (confusion)
- *"NOOOOOO!"* (tears)
- *"NO NO NO NO NO!"* (parent having breakdown)

But here's the paradox: The louder "no" gets, the less meaning it carries. It becomes pure emotion—scary sound from angry giant. The actual prohibition message gets lost in the emotional storm.

Meanwhile, a quiet, firm "no" with physical intervention (removing child from danger) builds understanding faster than any volume. But that requires us to actually get up from the couch, so...

The Positive No Building

Instead of just "no," build the universe:

Danger No: *"No touch—hot! Ouch!"* (connecting to sensation)

Social No: *"No yelling—sleeping baby"* (connecting to visible consequence)

Practical No: *"No throwing—breaks—all gone"* (connecting to permanence)

Arbitrary No: *"No drawing on walls—paper only"* (offering alternative)

You're not just prohibiting. You're constructing understanding one connection at a time. It only takes 847 repetitions.

Try This: The No Mapping

For one week, track every "no":
- What triggered it?
- What category was it? (safety/social/practical/arbitrary)
- Did child stop?
- Did it happen again?
- How many times today?
- Are you still sane?

You'll discover patterns:
- Safety nos work better (concrete consequence—fire hot)
- Social nos barely register (abstract concept—inside voice)
- Arbitrary nos never stick (no logical universe—don't jump on couch)
- Phone nos are ignored (they know you need it more than they do)

The Laughing Response

When toddlers laugh at "no," parents see defiance. But laughter is often confusion or anxiety:

- Unexpected sound from parent (nervous laugh)
- Don't understand but parent's face is funny (social laugh)
- Think it's a game (play laugh)
- Overwhelmed by prohibition (stress laugh)
- Genuinely find your frustration hilarious (problem)

They're not mocking your authority. They literally don't understand that authority exists as a concept. To them, you're just the large person who provides snacks and makes interesting sounds when they touch things.

The Testing Theory Myth

"They're testing boundaries!" Not really. Testing requires:
- Understanding boundaries exist
- Knowing they can be moved
- Strategic thinking
- Future planning
- Cause-effect comprehension
- Manipulation skills
- Tiny lab coat (optional)

A two-year-old touching the forbidden object while looking at you isn't testing. They're trying to understand:
- Will the sound happen again?
- Is the sound connected to my action?
- Does the sound mean something?
- Is this a pattern?
- Why is your face turning purple?

It's science, not defiance. They're basically tiny researchers with terrible methodology and no ethical oversight.

The Generalization Failure

"I've told them no hitting a thousand times!" But each time was different:

- No hitting sister
- No hitting at school
- No hitting with toys
- No hitting when angry
- No hitting the dog
- No hitting yourself
- No hitting daddy (unless playing)
- No hitting the piñata (wait, yes hitting the piñata)

To an adult, these are all "hitting." To a child, these are completely separate actions in different universes. The abstract category "hitting" that encompasses all striking motions regardless of context, target, or motivation—that doesn't exist yet.

The piñata really throws them.
"Hit this paper animal with a stick for candy!"
"But no hitting?"
"This hitting is okay!"
"..."
Universe exploded.

The Word-Action Disconnect

Young children often seem to process 'no' as just a sound rather than a directive. Watch:

Parent: *"No throwing!"*
Child: (throws)
Parent: *"I said NO THROWING!"*
Child: *"No throwing!"* (while throwing)

The child has learned to repeat the sounds. They haven't connected those sounds to stopping their body. It's like they're operating on two separate channels—the word channel and the body channel—and these channels don't communicate. Like cable news networks.

Building Categories

Help them construct "no" categories

Hot Things (danger category):
- Stove is hot-no
- Oven is hot-no
- Coffee is hot-no
- Iron is hot-no
- Pattern: Hot things are always no
- Except cocoa (hot-yes?)
- Universe confused again

Hurting (social category):
- Hitting hurts-no
- Pushing hurts-no
- Biting hurts-no
- Pinching hurts-no
- Pattern: Hurting is always no
- Except shots at doctor (hurting-yes?)
- Except removing splinters (hurting-necessary?)

You're not just saying no. You're building categorical understanding. With many exceptions that break the categories. Good luck.

The Replacement Strategy

"No" creates a vacuum. Young brains abhor vacuums.

Instead of: *"No standing on the couch"*
Try: *"Feet on floor"* or *"Sit on couch"* or *"Couches are for sitting"*

Instead of: *"No grabbing"*
Try: *"Gentle hands"* or *"Wait your turn"* or *"Ask first"*

Instead of: *"No screaming"*
Try: *"Quiet voice"* or *"Tell me with words"* or *"Scream outside"*

You're filling the vacuum with actionable alternatives. Except now they're screaming outside. Still technically compliance.

The Visual No

For children under 4, visual "no" works better than verbal:

- Red circles with lines through actions
- Shaking head while saying no
- Removing object from reach
- Physically blocking action

Their visual processing is stronger than auditory. Show "no" don't just say it.

The No Economy

Some families try the "limited no" approach:

- Only 5 "no"s per day
- Must be important
- Everything else gets positive redirection

Day 1: *"No touching the—"* (child runs into traffic)
"NO NO NO NO!" All five nos used in one emergency.
Rest of day: Chaos.

Turns out rationing "no" is like rationing breathing. Theoretically possible, practically disastrous.

The Developmental Timeline

12-18 months: *"No"* is interesting sound
- Might pause when hearing it
- No real comprehension
- Need physical intervention
- Will definitely do the thing

18-24 months: *"No"* means *"parent is making noise"*
- Sometimes stop briefly
- Resume quickly
- Starting to connect sound to action
- Still do the thing while saying "no"

2-3 years: *"No"* means *"stop current action"*
- Will stop momentarily
- Don't generalize
- Need constant repetition
- Eye contact while doing prohibited thing

3-4 years: *"No"* starting to categorize
- Beginning to understand types
- Still very literal
- Can't project forward
- Argue about technical definitions

4-5 years: *"No"* becoming conceptual
- Starting to generalize
- Understanding some categories
- Beginning prediction
- Loophole detection activated

5-7 years: *"No"* mostly understood
- Categories forming
- Can project forward
- Starting to self-regulate
- Professional loophole detection

8+: *"No"* fully understood
- Choose to ignore it
- Different problem entirely
- Good luck

The Sibling No Transfer

Fascinating phenomenon: Older sibling learns "no markers on walls." Younger sibling watches older get in trouble. Younger sibling immediately draws on walls with crayons.

> *"But you just saw what happened!"*
> *"Those were markers. These are crayons."*
> Technically correct. The most frustrating kind of correct.

They're not being defiant. They haven't generalized "no drawing implements on walls." They learned "no markers on walls." Crayons are clearly different. As are pens, pencils, paint, food.

What This Means

When a two-year-old ignores "no," they're not defying you. They're operating without the categorical, temporal, and conceptual universes that make "no" meaningful.

Understanding this transforms discipline from a power struggle to universe construction. You're not fighting their will. You're building their understanding, one category at a time, one exhausting repetition at a time.

The child who "knows better"? They know in one very specific context that doesn't transfer to the current situation. The child who laughs at "no"? They're confused, not disrespectful. The child who does it anyway while looking at you? They're conducting research, not planning your demise.

Probably.

CHAPTER 15

The Question Universe
("Why?")

"Why is the sky blue?"
"Because of light scattering."
"Why?"
"Because molecules in the air scatter blue light."
"Why?"
"Because... that's how light works."
"Why?"
"Because... physics?"
"Why?"
"Because... the universe... exists?"
"Why?"

Every parent knows this spiral. But here's what could be happening: "Why" isn't really a question. It's a universe-building tool. It's cognitive construction equipment. This could be your child literally assembling reality, one annoying question at a time.

The Connection Machine

Each "why" is the child trying to connect one small universe to another:

- The universe of *"sky"*
- The universe of *"blue"*
- The universe of *"because"*
- The universe of *"light"*
- The universe of cause and effect
- The universe of parent slowly losing sanity

They're not trying to drive you crazy. They're literally constructing reality, one connection at a time. It's just that reality has a lot of connections. Like, infinite connections. And they want to understand all of them. Right now. At bedtime.

Think of it like this: You're looking at a completed puzzle. They have a pile of pieces. Each "why" is them holding up two pieces, asking "Do these connect? How? Where? Can I eat this piece?"

The Different Whys

Not all "whys" are the same:

The Information Why: *"Why do we eat?"*
- Actually seeking information
- Will listen to answer
- Satisfied with explanation
- Rare as unicorns

The Connection Why: *"Why is grass green?"*
- Testing if things relate
- Answer less important than connection
- May not listen to response
- Just confirming universe has patterns

The Delay Why: *"Why do I have to go to bed?"*
- Stalling tactic
- Already knows answer
- Will ask regardless of response
- Can continue indefinitely

The Attention Why: *"Why? Why? Why? Why?"*
- Seeking interaction
- Content irrelevant
- Connection is the goal
- Parent interaction is the answer

The Anxiety Why: *"Why did grandma die?"*
- Seeking comfort
- Needs emotion not information
- Will repeat despite answers
- Hug required, PhD in philosophy optional

Learning to recognize which "why" you're dealing with changes your response strategy. And sanity level.

The Broken Record Phenomenon

"I already told you why!"

But they're not asking the same question. Each "why" digs deeper:

"Why do I have to wear shoes?"
(Level 1: Rule) *"Because it protects your feet."*

"Why?"
(Level 2: Protection concept) *"Because the ground can hurt."*

"Why?"
(Level 3: Pain causation) *"Because there might be sharp things."*

"Why?"
(Level 4: Object existence) *"Because... things exist that are sharp."*

"Why?"
(Level 5: Nature of reality) *"Because atoms form molecular structures that—"*

"Why?"
"BECAUSE I SAID SO!"
"Why do you say so?"
(Parent walks into ocean)

They've gone from shoes to existential philosophy in five questions. It's like conversational parkour, except you're tired and they have infinite energy.

Try This: The Why Mapping

Next time the why spiral starts, write down each question. You'll see they're not repetitions—they're excavations. Each why digs into a different layer of understanding.

Child: *"Why do we eat?"*
You: *"To get energy"*
MAP: [eating] connects to [energy]

Child: *"Why do we need energy?"*
You: *"To move and play"*
MAP: [energy] connects to [movement]

Child: *"Why do we move?"*
You: *"To do things"*
MAP: [movement] connects to [purpose]

Child: *"Why do we do things?"*
You: *"To... live life?"*
MAP: [purpose] connects to [existence]

Child: *"Why do we exist?"*
You: *"Let's have a snack"*
MAP: [existence] connects to [avoiding philosophy with 4-year-old]

They're building a universe map, one connection at a time. You're trying to remain sane, one snack at a time.

The Existential Crisis Why

Around age 4-5, the whys get heavy:

> *"Why do people die?"*
> *"Why can't I fly?"*
> *"Why was I born?"*
> *"Why is there nighttime?"*
> *"Why can't toys be real?"*
> *"Why can't I have ice cream for breakfast?"*
> *"Why do you look so tired?"*

These aren't random. The child is discovering limitations—of body, of reality, of existence, of parental patience. Each "why" is them processing that the universe has rules they can't break.

Your instinct is to give comforting answers. But they're not seeking comfort—they're seeking structure. "That's how the world works" is often more satisfying than elaborate explanations.

> *"Why can't I fly?"*
> *"Humans don't have wings."*
> *"Why?"*
> *"Evolution didn't give us wings."*
> *"Why?"*
> *"We developed big brains instead."*
> *"Why?"*
> *"To ask why questions apparently."*

The Social Why

"Why can't I hit him?"
"Because it hurts."
"Why?"
"Because bodies feel pain."
"Why?"
"Because we have nerves."
"Why?"
"Because that's how we know if we're hurt."
"Why?"
"So we can protect ourselves."
"Why?"
"So we survive."
"Why?"
"SO OUR SPECIES CONTINUES AND SOMEONE
CAN KEEP ASKING WHY!"

They're not questioning the rule. They're trying to understand the invisible social physics that govern interaction. Why does hitting equal bad? It's not obvious if you're four. Hitting gets you the toy. Seems effective.

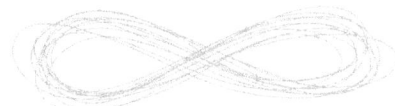

The Recursive Why Loop

Sometimes children get stuck in why loops:

"Why is water wet?"
"That's what makes it water."
"Why?"
"Because wet is how water feels."
"Why?"
"Because water molecules move freely."
"Why?"
"Because they're not frozen."
"Why?"
"Because it's not cold enough."
"Why is it not cold enough?"
"Because it's summer."
"Why is it summer?"
"Earth's axial tilt and orbital position."
"Why?"
"Because of gravitational forces during planetary formation 4.5 billion years ago."
"Why?"
"Because of the Big Bang."
"Why?"
"Nobody knows."
"Why?"
"BECAUSE NOBODY KNOWS WHY!"
"Why don't they know?"
(Parent hides in pantry)

This isn't defiance. They've hit a foundational reality that can't be explained further. Like asking why 1 equals 1. Some things just ARE, but that's an unsatisfying answer to a universe-building brain.

The Because Problem

Adult "because" contains cause and effect.
Child "because" is just a connecting word.

Listen to a four-year-old explain something:

"We went to the store because and then because we got ice cream because it was Tuesday because mom said because the dog because because because."

They're using "because" as "and then"—a sequence connector, not a causation indicator. When you answer their why with because, they might just be hearing "and then something else happens for mysterious reasons."

The Answer Immunity

"Why do I have to clean up?"
"Because I said so."
"Why?"
"Because I'm the parent."
"Why?"
"Because... I gave birth to you."
"Why?"
"Because daddy and I decided to have children."
"Why?"

"Because I said so" doesn't work because it's not a universe connection. It's a power assertion. The child isn't challenging authority—they literally don't understand how "parent saying" connects to "child doing."

Try This: The Connection Answer

Instead of authority-based answers, build connections:

"Why do I have to clean up?"

"Toys on the floor might break or get lost. You want to play with them tomorrow, right?"

You've connected:
- Current action (cleaning)
- To future state (tomorrow's play)
- Through consequence (breaking/losing)

That's a universe connection they can process. It might take 47 more whys to fully understand, but it's a start.

The Peak Why Period

Why questions peak between ages 3.5 and 4.5. If a typical four-year-old asks, let's say 300+ questions per day (give or take, usually give). That could be as many as one every 2-3 minutes of waking hours.

Let's do the math:
- 300 questions per day
- 14 waking hours
- 21 questions per hour
- 1 question every 2.8 minutes
- 2,100 questions per week
- 109,500 questions per year
- Your sanity: Gone by Tuesday

This isn't random. It's when:
- Language explodes
- Causation understanding emerges
- Social rules become visible
- Physical laws get noticed
- Limitations become apparent

Their brain is in universe-building overdrive. Every why is a construction project.

The Car Why Phenomenon

Something about being strapped in a car seat activates Maximum Why Mode:

"Why are we stopping?"
"Red light."
"Why?"
"So cars don't crash."
"Why would they crash?"
"Because they'd hit each other."
"Why?"
"Because they're going different directions."
"Why?"
"Because people need to go different places."
"Why?"
"Because we don't all live in the same house."
"Why?"
"Because there are too many people."
"Why are there too many people?"
"Ask your dad."

"Why?"
"Because mommy needs quiet now."
"Why?"
"Because mommy's eye is twitching."
"Why is your eye twitching?"

You're trapped. They know you're trapped. The questions will continue until you reach your destination.

The Emotional Why

"Why are you sad?"
"Because I'm tired."
"Why?"
"Because I didn't sleep well."
"Why?"
"Because I was worried."
"Why?"
"Because of adult things."
"Why?"
"Because adults worry about money and health and the future and—"
"Why?"
"Because that's what adults do."
"Why?"
"I DON'T KNOW, IT JUST HAPPENED WHEN I TURNED 30!"

These aren't information searches. The child is trying to understand emotional causation—that feelings have triggers, that triggers have sources, that adults have interior worlds that are apparently full of anxiety.

The Shutdown Strategy

When you're exhausted from whys:

The Reverse: *"Why do YOU think?"* (Buys you 30 seconds)

The Delay: *"Good question. Let's think about that during bath time."* (They'll forget)

The Demonstration: *"Let's find out!"* (Google becomes your best friend)

The Companion Why: *"I don't know. Why do you think clouds are white?"* (Mutual confusion)

The Honest Limit: *"My brain is too tired for whys. Let's do them tomorrow."* (Tomorrow you'll be tired too, but that's tomorrow's problem)

The Emergency Eject: *"Look, a squirrel!"* (60% success rate)

You're not shutting down learning. You're managing your own universe-building capacity. Even construction workers get breaks.

What This Means

The why phase isn't a phase—it's architecture. They're building the entire structure of reality, one connection at a time.

When we understand this:
- We see questions as construction, not annoyance
- We provide connections, not just answers
- We recognize the exhausting importance
- We protect our own energy while honoring theirs
- We hide in the bathroom sometimes

That endless "why?" isn't defiance or manipulation. It's a small human building their universe, one question at a time. And you're the construction supervisor whether you signed up or not.

The child who won't stop asking why? They're not trying to drive you crazy. They're trying to build reality. And reality, it turns out, requires a LOT of connections.

Approximately, An infinite number per year. But who's counting?

(You are. You're definitely counting, good luck with that.)

PART V

Different Contexts, Different Children

CHAPTER 16

The Restaurant Reality

At home, your four-year-old sits nicely at dinner. At a restaurant, they're a disaster. What happened?

Different context, different universe.

At home, "sit for dinner" means:
- In my special chair
- With my usual plate
- Can get up for potty
- Can play with toys after
- Parents relaxed and chatting
- Normal volume is fine
- Escape route available

At a restaurant, "sit for dinner" means:
- In strange chair that might move
- With breakable things everywhere
- Can't get up even for potty without production

- No toys visible anywhere
- Parents tense and whispering
- Must modulate volume mysteriously
- Strange people watching
- Weird smells and sounds
- Food takes forever to appear
- Can't eat the bread all at once?
- Have to sit still even AFTER eating?
- What do you mean we can't leave yet?
- The check? What check? This is torture!

It's not the same universe at all. It's universe vertigo. It's expecting someone to perform their normal morning routine while skydiving.

The Sensory Assault Map

Let's map what's actually happening in a restaurant through a child's sensory system:

Visual Overload:
- Fluorescent or dim lighting (can't regulate)
- Movement in peripheral vision constantly
- Shiny surfaces creating glare
- Too many faces to track
- Menu with incomprehensible symbols
- Food that looks different than home version
- Other kids eating things they can't have
- Dessert case mocking them
- TVs everywhere showing sports (why?)

Auditory Chaos:
- Multiple conversations at equal volume
- Kitchen noises (crashes, sizzles, beeps)

- Music competing with voices
- Echo from hard surfaces
- Chair scraping sounds
- Their own voice sounds different
- Someone's baby crying (contagious)
- Birthday song at another table (where's MY cake?)
- Blender sounds like monster

Olfactory Confusion:
- Competing food smells
- Cleaning product smell
- Other people's perfume
- Bathroom smell wafting over
- Their food smells wrong
- Something burning somewhere
- Fish (always fish, even at pizza places)

Tactile Distress:
- Sticky table
- Cold chair
- Scratchy napkin
- Heavy silverware
- Wet spots from previous diners
- Air conditioning creating temperature chaos
- Vinyl seats that make noise when you move
- Fork is wrong size for mouth
- Everything slightly greasy

Vestibular Disruption:
- Chair too high/low
- Feet don't touch ground
- Table wrong height
- Can't move to regulate
- Sitting still too long
- Booth that swallows them
- Wobbly table (parent trying to fix with napkins)

That's five sensory systems in overload simultaneously. No wonder they melt down. They're basically being waterboarded by ambiance.

The Waiting Universe

Adults understand restaurant waiting:

- Order taken (5-10 minutes)
- Food prepared (15-20 minutes)
- Eating time (30-40 minutes)
- Bill and departure (10 minutes)
- Total time investment calculated
- Phone available for distraction

Children experience:

- Sitting (FOREVER)
- Still sitting (ETERNITY)
- STILL SITTING WHY?
- Food appears (TOO LATE, ALREADY DEAD)
- Have to keep sitting (RESURRECTION INTO MORE SITTING)
- Still can't leave (WHAT IS THIS?)

Without time comprehension, waiting is torture. Every minute is unexpected, unending, unbearable. It's like being told "we'll leave eventually" while in prison.

Try This: The Restaurant Prep Kit

Create a restaurant survival kit:

- Visual timer (shows time passing)
- Quiet activities (change weekly for novelty)
- Sensory tools (fidget, chenille stem, quiet things)
- Snack for emergencies (prevents hanger meltdown)

- Comfort object (small, discrete)
- Tablet with headphones (judge away, judgy parents)
- Backup outfit (for inevitable spills)

Don't bring it out immediately. Use strategically when you see universe collapse approaching. Like an emergency parachute for their sanity. And yours.

The Performance Pressure

At home, eating is eating. At restaurants, eating is performance.

Parents suddenly care about:
- Napkin placement
- Elbow position
- Volume control
- Sitting still
- *"Please"* and *"thank you"* frequency
- Not staring at other diners
- Inside voice (what happened to home voice?)
- Not eating with hands (but home pizza?)
- Not mixing foods (but home everything-bowl?)
- Chewing with mouth closed (impossible with giant fork)

The child is trying to:
- Navigate sensory overload
- Manage hunger
- Process new environment
- AND perform *"good behavior"*
- While their brain is shutting down
- And you keep making angry eyes

It's like asking them to juggle while learning algebra during a fire drill in a foreign language.

The Social Universe Collision

Restaurant rules are different from EVERY other social universe:

STORE: Can walk around, touch things sometimes
RESTAURANT: Must sit, can't explore

LIBRARY: Quiet voices, can get up for books
RESTAURANT: Quiet voices, can't get up at all

HOME: Eat when hungry
RESTAURANT: Wait even if starving

PLAYGROUND: Run, yell, move freely
RESTAURANT: Opposite of everything playground taught

SCHOOL: Raise hand, wait turn
RESTAURANT: How do I get water? HELLO?

Every social universe they've learned actively contradicts restaurant universe. They're not being bad. They're confused about which universe they're in and why this one is horrible.

The Hunger Amplification Effect

By the time you get to a restaurant:

- Decision to go (30 minutes ago)
- Getting ready (15 minutes)
- Arguing about shoes (10 minutes)
- Driving there (15 minutes)
- Waiting for table (10 minutes)
- Being seated (5 minutes)
- Ordering (10 minutes)
- Food preparation (20 minutes)

That's 1.5-2 hours from "let's eat" to actual food. For a young child, that's a physiological crisis. Their blood sugar has crashed, their universe-building capacity is gone, and you're asking for peak performance.

It's like running a marathon then being asked to perform Swan Lake.

The Menu Meltdown

"What do you want to eat?" (Shows menu with 47 options)

Child's brain:
- Can't read
- Pictures don't look like food
- Too many choices
- Don't know these words
- Want mac and cheese
- They don't have mac and cheese
- Everything is wrong
- Why are you asking me to make decisions
- I'm dying of hunger
- JUST FEED ME

"They have chicken fingers!"

"I don't want fingers!"

Valid concern, honestly.

The Family Style Disaster

"We'll all share!"

Sharing food at restaurants is universe collision:
- Home sharing: Informal, flexible
- Restaurant sharing: Formal, complex

Now add:
- Waiting for everyone to take some
- Not taking too much
- Not touching food you don't want
- Using serving spoons (not your fork)
- Managing disappointment when favorite runs out
- Watching dad eat all the good stuff
- Mom saying **"save some for others"**
- But dad didn't save any
- Family dynamics playing out over appetizers

That's five universes to coordinate while hungry.

Prevention Strategies That Actually Work

The Preview:
- Look at menu online first
- Choose food in advance
- Look at pictures of restaurant
- Discuss how it's different from home
- Set realistic expectations
- Prepare for disappointment
- Accept this might fail

The Timing Hack:
- Go at off-peak times (less sensory input)
- Or go right when they open (faster service)
- Never go when already hungry
- Pack car snacks for journey
- Feed them slightly before
- This is eating second dinner
- Accept your fate

The Position Strategy:
- Request booth (contains wiggly bodies)
- Or outside (more sensory regulation)
- Away from kitchen (less noise/smell)
- Corner table (fewer directions to monitor)
- Near exit (escape route visible)
- Far from bathroom (smell factor)
- Not near bar (drunk people are unpredictable)

The Order Hack:
- Order kids' meal immediately
- Or order appetizer that arrives fast
- Bring acceptable snack for waiting
- Order dessert with meal (prevents end waiting)
- Get everything to go (smartest option)

The Other Kids Comparison

"Look at that little girl sitting nicely!" That little girl might be:

- Older (by even 6 months)
- Temperamentally different
- Not hungry
- Experienced (goes weekly)
- On a device
- Medicated (not joking)
- Dead inside from restaurant training
- Actually a robot

Comparing children in restaurants is like comparing fish and birds at swimming. Different species, different capacities, different parental breaking points.

The Success Measurement

Success isn't "sat perfectly through formal dinner." Success might be:

- Stayed seated for 10 minutes
- Used inside voice once
- Didn't throw anything
- Tried new food (licked it counts)
- Made it to food arriving
- Only one meltdown
- Didn't trigger other tables' kids
- Left before complete collapse
- Nobody banned us
- We lived

Lower the bar to where your child can succeed, then lower it more.

The Recovery Protocol

When restaurant fails (and it will):

In the moment:
- One parent takes child outside
- Walk around building (movement regulates)
- Name what's happening (*"Too loud inside"*)
- Don't punish (universe collapse isn't defiance)
- Consider leaving (really, it's okay)

After:
- Debrief when calm
- *"What was hardest?"*
- Problem-solve together
- Try again with adjustments
- Or don't
- Takeout exists for a reason

Each attempt builds universe connections, even failures.

The Server Situation

Servers are either angels or complexity-adders:

Angel Server:
- Brings crackers immediately
- Speeds up kid order
- Doesn't judge
- Brings extra napkins without asking
- Understands the struggle
- Probably has kids
- Or teaches preschool
- Is actual saint

Complexity Server:
- Takes forever
- Asks child complicated questions
- Judges your parenting
- Forgets kid's food
- Brings hot plate to child
- Acts like your kid is problem
- Doesn't understand biology
- Makes everything worse

You can't control which you get. It's restaurant roulette.

The Developmental Timeline

Around age 2-3: 15-minute maximum
- Fast food only
- Bring all entertainment
- Expect to leave suddenly

Around age 4-5: 30 minutes possible
- Family restaurants
- Still need activities
- One course realistic
- Lower all expectations

Around age 6-7: 45 minutes emerging
- Can wait briefly
- Starting to understand
- Still need movement breaks
- Bribery still required

Around age 8-10: Full meal possible
- Can participate in conversation
- Understanding waiting
- Restaurant universe stabilizing

Around age 11+: Actually pleasant
- Real conversation possible
- Trying new foods
- Restaurant veterans
- Now they judge YOUR manners

What This Means

Restaurant disasters aren't behavior problems. They're universe problems. Your child isn't being bad at restaurants—they're experiencing universe vertigo while hungry, overwhelmed, confused, and trapped.

When we understand this:
- We prepare differently
- We choose restaurants strategically
- We adjust expectations to subterranean levels
- We respond with support, not shame
- We recognize survival as success
- We appreciate takeout
- We tip servers extra for patience

The child who "can't behave in restaurants" is actually a child whose brain is trying to navigate multiple universe collisions simultaneously while their blood sugar crashes and strangers judge their parents.

Once you see it, you can't unsee it.

And that changes everything about eating out with children.

CHAPTER 17

Digital Natives and the Swipe Generation

Some Modern children often learn "swipe," "tap," and "click" before "pour," "fold," or "tie." This creates parallel universes with incompatible physics.

In the digital universe:
- Mistakes vanish with "undo"
- Waiting is optional (skip ad)
- Everything responds instantly
- Restart fixes everything
- Attention can jump between multiple tabs
- Progress saves automatically
- Demise is temporary (respawn)
- Boredom is impossible (infinite content)
- If you don't like something, swipe away

In the physical universe:
- Spilled milk stays spilled
- Waiting is mandatory
- Some things never respond
- Breaking means broken
- Focus has to sustain
- Progress requires repetition
- Consequences are permanent
- Boredom is real
- You're stuck with what you have

When a four-year-old has a meltdown because they can't "restart" their broken cookie or "pause" their need to pee, they're not being irrational. They're experiencing universe collision. The rules they've learned most thoroughly (digital) don't apply to their current situation (physical).

It's like training for years to be a pilot then being told to drive a car with pilot controls. Nothing works the way your brain expects.

The Undo Generation

Watch a three-year-old who's spent significant time on tablets:
- **Breaks toy:** *"Fix it!"* (expecting restore function)
- **Spills juice:** *"Go back!"* (expecting undo)
- **Loses game:** *"Start over!"* (expecting reset)
- **Makes mistake:** *"Delete!"* (expecting erasure)
- **Hits sister:** *"Restart!"* (expecting clean slate)
- **Tears paper:** *"Control Z!"* (knows the shortcut)
- **Breaks crayon:** *"New one!"* (expecting infinite resources)

They're not spoiled. They're applying digital universe physics to physical reality. In their primary universe (screen), every mistake is reversible. The permanence of physical consequences is genuinely shocking.

"But we can't unbake the cookies."
"Why?"
"Because chemistry doesn't have undo."
"That's stupid."
Hard to argue, honestly.

The Instant Response Expectation

Digital natives expect immediate response because that's their primary universe:

DIGITAL: Touch screen → instant reaction
PHYSICAL: Push button → maybe something happens eventually

DIGITAL: Swipe → immediate new content
PHYSICAL: Turn page → same book continues

DIGITAL: Click → instant gratification
PHYSICAL: Ask → maybe wait → possibly receive → probably no

DIGITAL: Search → 1 million results in 0.3 seconds
PHYSICAL: "Where's my shoe?" → 30-minute investigation

When they have meltdowns about waiting, they're not impatient by nature. They're experiencing physics violation. In their primary universe, waiting doesn't exist. Everything is instant or skippable.

"Why can't we skip the car ride?"
"Physics."
"I hate physics."

The Attention Fragment Pattern

Apps are designed to capture attention in 3-second chunks:
- Bright reward
- Sound effect
- Visual stimulation
- Immediate next prompt
- Constant novelty
- Dopamine hit
- Repeat forever

Now ask this brain to:
- Listen to a story (minutes of sustained attention)
- Complete a puzzle (delayed gratification)
- Practice writing (repetitive, no rewards)
- Wait their turn (no stimulation)
- Sit through dinner (eternity of sameness)
- Sleep (THE ULTIMATE BOREDOM)

The contrast is devastating. It's not that they can't pay attention. They're paying attention in 3- second digital chunks in a world requiring 3-minute analog flows. Their brain is constantly looking for the next swipe opportunity in a world that doesn't swipe.

Try This: The Screen-to-Reality Bridge

After screen time, don't jump straight to analog activities. Build bridges:

1. Screen ends
2. Physical movement (3-5 minutes)
    *   Jump around
    *   Run outside
    *   Dance party
    *   Anything to reset
3. Sensory activity (playdough, water)
    *   Hands need to touch real things
    *   Brain needs non-screen input
4. Then attempt focused task

You're helping their brain shift physics systems gradually rather than crashing between universes. It's like decompression for divers, but for attention.

The Pause Impossibility

"Pause the game and come to dinner!"
"I CAN'T PAUSE!"
"YES YOU CAN!"
"IT'S ONLINE!"
"I DON'T CARE IF IT'S ONLINE!"
"BUT MY TEAM!"
"PAUSE IT NOW!"
Game character dies. Child cries. Parent feels guilty but also vindicated. Nobody wins.

Sometimes they literally can't pause (online games). But often, they're expressing something deeper: In the digital universe, they control time. In physical reality, time controls them.

The power to pause, save, and resume is intoxicating to a young brain that has no control over most of life. Returning to physical universe means surrendering that control. It's like being a time wizard who suddenly has to be mortal again.

The Multiple Lives Mindset

In games, failure is temporary:
- Die? Respawn
- Fail? Retry
- Mess up? Reload save
- Fall off cliff? Back in 3 seconds
- Game over? Not really

This creates a specific relationship with failure that crashes into physical reality:
- Break something? Can't respawn it
- Hurt someone? Can't reload save
- Fail at task? Can't just retry immediately
- Fall off bike? Actually hurt
- Friendship over? Might be really over

The permanence is paralyzing. They're not being careless. They're operating with digital universe assumptions about consequences.

"Why can't we respawn Goldfish?"
"Because death is permanent."
"That's bad game design."
Can't argue with that logic.

The Notification Brain

Modern apps train brains for constant interruption:
- Ding! New message
- Buzz! Achievement unlocked
- Pop! Someone liked your creation
- Swoosh! Daily reward ready
- Bloop! Friend online
- Zing! Update available
- EVERYTHING NEEDS ATTENTION NOW

This builds a brain that expects and needs constant
external validation and stimulation. Then we ask them to:
- Play alone quietly
- Entertain themselves
- Focus without feedback
- Find intrinsic motivation
- Appreciate silence
- Exist without constant input

They're not addicted to screens. Their brains have been architected for a universe of constant external input. Asking them to operate without it is like asking someone to breathe without air.

The Tutorial Expectation

Every game starts with a tutorial:
- Explicit instructions
- Practice mode
- Visual guides
- Immediate feedback
- Progressive difficulty
- Hint button always available
- Can repeat if needed

Real life offers:
- Vague instructions
- No practice mode
- Figure it out yourself
- Delayed or no feedback
- Random difficulty spikes
- No hints
- One chance only
- Good luck

When a child expects explicit instruction for everything, they're not helpless. They're expecting tutorial mode. Life doesn't have one.

"Where's the tutorial for making friends?"
"There isn't one."
"This game sucks."

The Score Visibility Problem

In games, progress is always visible:
- Points accumulating
- Levels advancing
- Achievements unlocking
- Progress bars filling
- XP gaining
- Stats increasing
- Rank rising

In life, progress is invisible:

- Learning happens imperceptibly
- Growth is gradual
- Achievement is subjective
- Progress is unmeasurable
- No XP bar
- No level ups
- No achievement notifications

A child practicing writing doesn't see a progress bar. They just see bad letters, then more bad letters, then still bad letters. No wonder they think they're not improving.

Try This: Make Progress Visible

Create real-world progress bars:

- Sticker charts (visual achievements)
- Before/after photos of skills
- Video progress over time
- Counting successful attempts
- Celebrating micro-improvements
- *"Level up"* celebrations
- Actual progress bars on wall

You're translating physical universe progress into digital universe visibility. It's achievement unlocking for reality.

The Filter Reality Distortion

Filters and effects teach that reality is instantly changeable:
- Don't like your face? Filter
- Room too messy? Background swap
- Drawing looks bad? Auto-enhance
- Voice sounds weird? Voice changer
- Too dark? Brightness up
- Don't like the photo? Take 50 more instantly

Physical reality is unfiltered, unenhanced, unchangeable:
- Your face is your face
- Messy room stays messy
- Bad drawing stays bad
- Your voice is your voice
- Dark is dark
- Bad photo with film? Too bad, that was expensive

When a six-year-old has a meltdown because their drawing doesn't look like the tutorial, they're expecting an enhance function that doesn't exist.

The Social Universe Collision

Digital social interaction:
- Mute annoying people
- Block mean ones
- Leave when bored
- Find new friends instantly
- Avatar represents you
- Can be anyone
- Reputation resets with new account

Physical social interaction:
- Can't mute classmate
- Can't block sibling
- Can't leave classroom
- Same kids every day
- Your actual face represents you
- You're stuck being you
- Reputation follows forever

The digital universe gives control over social interaction that physical universe denies. School becomes torture when you can't log off.

"Can I block Tyler?"
"No, he's in your class."
"Can I mute him?"
"No."
"Can I unfriend him?"
"You're not friends."
"Then why do I have to see him?"
"Because... society."
"Society needs better settings."

The YouTube Reality Distortion

Kids watch YouTube where:
- Everything is edited
- Boring parts cut out
- Multiple takes for perfection
- Instant success shown
- Failures rarely included
- 10 minutes looks easy
- Everyone's amazing at everything

Then they try the same thing:
- No editing
- All boring parts included
- One take only
- Failure immediate
- Success nowhere in sight
- Takes hours
- They're terrible at it

"Why doesn't mine look like YouTube?"
"Because they practiced for years and edited for hours."
"That's cheating!"
"That's marketing."

Building Bridge Universes

Help children navigate between universes:

Time Bridges: *"In games we can pause. In life, we use timers to know when to stop."*

Consequence Bridges: *"In games we restart. In life, we fix or learn from mistakes."*

Attention Bridges: *"Games give points. In life, we notice our own improvement."*

Social Bridges: *"Online we can leave. In person, we learn to work through problems."*

Reality Bridges: *"YouTube is edited. Real life includes all the messy parts."*

You're not demonizing digital or glorifying physical. You're acknowledging both universes and building connections.

The Generation Gap Reversal

For the first time in history, children are native speakers of a universe adults immigrated to. They're not being difficult when they expect digital physics in physical space. They're being native speakers.

This reversal means:

- Children know things adults don't
- Adult experience doesn't always apply
- Traditional wisdom might be obsolete
- Parents are immigrants in their children's primary universe
- Kids teach parents technology
- Parents teach kids reality
- Everyone's confused

What This Means

Digital native children aren't broken, addicted, or ruined. They're bilingual in universe systems, with digital as their first language.

When we understand this:

- We stop fighting their digital nature
- We build bridges between universes
- We translate rather than condemn
- We help them code-switch
- We recognize the challenge
- We admit we don't fully understand their world

The child melting down because they can't "restart" their broken cookie isn't spoiled. They're experiencing physics vertigo between incompatible universes.

The child who can't focus on homework but can game for hours isn't lazy. They're operating in different attention economies.

The child who expects instant everything isn't entitled. They're native to a universe where instant is normal.

Once you see it this way, your response changes from frustration to translation. And that changes everything about raising digital natives in an analog world.

Even if you still don't understand why they need to watch someone else play video games on YouTube while playing their own video game. That's meta-universe stuff. Nobody understands that.

PART VI

Building Bridges

CHAPTER 18

The Time Universe

"We'll go to the park in a minute." Meltdown in 3... 2... 1...

Here's why: *"Minute"* means nothing to a three-year-old. Neither does *"soon," "later," "in a while,"* or *"after."* These aren't just vague to them—they're literally meaningless. Time is an abstract universe they won't fully map until around age 7 or 8.

To you, time words create a mental timeline:
- Now
- In a minute (60 seconds)
- Soon (5-30 minutes)
- Later (hours)
- Tomorrow (next day)
- Next week (7 days)
- Eventually (undefined but finite)

To a three-year-old:

- Now (exists)
- Not now (doesn't exist)

That's it. Two categories. Everything else is "not now," whether it's five seconds or five days away. Time is binary. It either IS or ISN'T. There's no between.

The Now/Not-Now Binary

Young children live in a universe of only two time states. Watch what happens:

> *"We'll get ice cream later."*
> *Child hears: Ice cream! (later doesn't register)*
> *Ten seconds pass. "Is it later yet?"*
> *"No, later."*
> *"Now?"*
> *"No."*
> *"...Now?"*
> *"NO."*
> *"How about now?"*
> *"LATER MEANS LATER!"*
> *"When's later?"*
> *"AFTER DINNER!"*
> *"When's dinner?"*
> (Parent screams internally)

They're not being annoying. In their universe, you said ice cream exists. They can't gauge when "later" arrives because "later" is just "not now"—and now it's a new now, so maybe it's later?

The Tomorrow Problem

"Tomorrow" might be the most painful word in parenting:

What you mean: The day following this one, after you sleep and wake up

What they hear: Not now (could be anything)

What they experience: Existential void of waiting

"We'll go to grandma's tomorrow."
Bedtime: *"Are we going to grandma's now?"*
"No, tomorrow."

Middle of night: *"Is it tomorrow?"*
"No, still today."

3 AM: *"Tomorrow yet?"*
"GO TO SLEEP!"

5 AM: *"Now tomorrow?"*
"Technically yes but not time to go."

"BUT YOU SAID TOMORROW!"
MELTDOWN.

You said tomorrow. It's tomorrow. Why aren't we going? Because "tomorrow" and "tomorrow morning at 10 AM after breakfast and getting dressed" are vastly different universes.

The Routine Time Anchor

Children often struggle with telling time, but they can sequence. This is why routine is sanity:

Abstract: *"Dinner is at 6 PM"*
Concrete: *"Dinner is after Dad comes home"*

Abstract: *"Bedtime in an hour"*
Concrete: *"Bedtime after two more shows"*

Abstract: *"We leave in 20 minutes"*
Concrete: *"We leave after you finish that puzzle"*

They can't measure time, but they can track events. Use this. Anchor everything to something concrete.

Try This: The Event Chain

Instead of time words, create event chains:

"First breakfast, then get dressed, then brush teeth, then school."
Draw it out:

Now they can see where they are in the sequence. "Two more things until school" means something. "Twenty minutes" means nothing.

Make it visual. Make it concrete. Make it survivable.

The Waiting Torture

Waiting without markers is psychological torture for children:

Adult waiting: Mental time estimation, distraction, patience, phone scrolling

Child waiting: Eternal present moment of want without fulfillment

"Wait a minute" to a child feels like you feel when the WiFi is loading. That spinning circle with no progress bar? That's their entire experience of waiting. Except they can't check Twitter to pass the time.

This is why:
- Car rides feel eternal (no progress markers)
- *"Five more minutes"* of play feels like two seconds (absorbed in now)
- Waiting rooms are called waiting rooms (they're torture chambers)
- Checkout lines create meltdowns (candy at child height is evil)

The Birthday Time Warp

"My birthday is in two months!"

To an adult: Short time, plan party, order cake
To a five-year-old: Infinite meaningless void
Then suddenly:
"Is today my birthday?"
"No."
"Is TODAY my birthday?"
"Still no."
"How about now?"
Every. Single. Day.

They're not obsessed. They literally cannot judge the passage of two months. It might as well be two centuries. So they check daily if the mysterious future event has suddenly become now.

"How many sleeps until my birthday?"
"Sixty."
"Is that a lot?"
"Yes."
"More than ten?"
"Yes."
"I can't count that high."
"I know."
"So it's never?"
"Basically."

The Speed Perception Problem

Time moves at different speeds for children:

FUN TIME: Accelerated (park visit = 5 minutes subjectively)
BORING TIME: Frozen (car ride = 5 hours subjectively)
WAITING TIME: Reversed (actually gets longer)
SCREEN TIME: Nonexistent (what do you mean it's been 2 hours?)
HOMEWORK TIME: Geological (each math problem = lifetime)

This isn't perception—it's neurological. Their brain doesn't have the time-tracking apparatus yours does. They're experiencing time through engagement level, not chronological measurement.

"We were only at the park for five minutes!"
"It was two hours."
"NO!"

They genuinely believe you're not telling them the truth. In their experience, it WAS five minutes.

The Schedule Collision

"But you said we'd go to the park!"
"I said maybe, if we have time."
"You PROMISED!"
"I said we'll see."
"THAT'S A PROMISE!"

You didn't promise. You said conditional time words. But they heard "Park exists in future" which became "Park will happen" which became "Park is promised" which became betrayal when it didn't happen.

Conditional time doesn't exist in their universe. Things either will happen (promised) or won't happen (no). "Maybe" gets sorted into one of these categories, usually "yes."

> *"We'll see"* = Yes
> *"Maybe"* = Yes
> *"Possibly"* = Yes
> *"If we have time"* = Yes
> *"Probably not"* = Yes but quieter
> *"Absolutely not"* = Maybe

The Bedtime Time Warp

Why does bedtime take forever? Time dilation:

> 7:00 PM: *"Bedtime in 30 minutes"* (meaningless)
> 7:15 PM: *"15 more minutes"* (still meaningless)
> 7:25 PM: *"5 more minutes"* (panic—sudden time awareness)
> 7:30 PM: *"Bedtime!"* (shock—time jumped forward)
> 7:31 PM: *"I need water"* (time reversal attempt)
> 7:35 PM: *"I'm not tired"* (denying time exists)
> 7:40 PM: *"One more story"* (bargaining with time)
> 7:45 PM: *"I forgot to tell you something"* (time loop)
> 8:00 PM: Still not in bed (time has lost all meaning)
> 8:30 PM: Finally asleep (parent has aged 5 years)

They're not stalling (well, not just stalling). Their time universe is collapsing as they get tired, making time comprehension impossible.

Try This: The Bedtime Timer

Visual timers change everything:

- Red disk disappears as time passes
- Child can SEE time moving
- No surprise when time runs out
- Argues with timer, not you
- Timer is impartial judge

You've made abstract time visible. It's like giving them time-vision glasses. They still hate bedtime, but at least they can see it coming.

The Yesterday/Last Week Confusion

Ask a four-year-old when something happened:

"When did we go to the zoo?"
"Yesterday!"
"That was last month."
"Yesterday!"
"We went in October."
"YESTERDAY!"

Everything that happened before now is "yesterday."
They have:

- Now
- Not now (future)
- Before now (all collapsed into "yesterday")

Your wedding? Yesterday. Dinosaurs? Yesterday. This morning? Yesterday. Five minutes ago? Still yesterday.

Time is flat. Everything that already happened exists in the same temporal space called "yesterday."

The Age Time Distortion

"When will I be five?"
"In six months."
"How long is that?"
"180 days."
"Is that tomorrow?"
"No, many tomorrows."
"Three tomorrows?"
"More."
"Four?"
"Way more."
"Infinity tomorrows?"
"Not quite that many."
"So never."
"Not never."
"Yesterday?"
(Parent gives up)

Age changes are particularly painful because they combine:

- Abstract time measurement (months/years)
- Identity transformation (becoming different)
- Social significance (big kid status)
- Comparison pressure (friend is already five)

The question "When will I be bigger?" is existential. They're asking when they'll transform, and you're giving them measurements they can't process.

The Season Confusion

"When is Christmas?"
"In winter."
"When is winter?"
"In three months."
"Is that tomorrow?"
"No."
"The tomorrow after tomorrow?"
"No."
"All the tomorrows?"
"Some of them."
"So... yesterday?"
"How did you get to yesterday??"
"Time is confusing."

Seasons are time containers many children find difficult to grasp. They remember Christmas happened. They know it will happen again. But when? The calendar is meaningless. Months are meaningless.

They're trapped in an eternal now, knowing Christmas exists somewhere in the not-now, checking daily if it has suddenly appeared.

The Time Travel Fantasy

Children often believe they can change past events:

"I don't want to have spilled my juice!"
"But you did spill it."
"Make it not spilled!"
"I can't change the past."

"Why?"
"Time doesn't work that way."
"Time is broken."

They're not being irrational. In their universe, if something exists in "yesterday," and yesterday is just "not now," why can't we change it? The permanence of the past is incomprehensible when time is just now/not-now.

Building Time Comprehension

Around ages 2-3: Only now/not-now
- Use immediate sequences
- *"After this song"*
- Visual cues
- Everything is *"yesterday"* or *"tomorrow"*

Around ages 4-5: Event sequences emerging
- *"After lunch"*
- *"When daddy comes home"*
- Count sleeps, not days
- Still can't judge duration

Around ages 6-7: Duration understanding beginning
- Can use timers
- Understand "longer" and "shorter"
- Still can't estimate well
- Think 5 minutes and 5 hours are similar

Around ages 8-9: Abstract time emerging
- Can use clocks meaningfully
- Understand weeks/months
- Can plan ahead
- Still optimistic about homework time

Around ages 10+: Full time universe online
- Can estimate duration
- Understand abstract future
- Can delay gratification
- Still late for everything

What This Means

When a child melts down about time, they're not being impatient. They're experiencing existence without temporal framework. Imagine living without any sense of how long things take, when things will happen, or how much time has passed.

That's childhood.

When we understand this:

- We use concrete anchors, not abstract time
- We make time visible when possible
- We recognize waiting as torture
- We stop saying "soon" and "later"
- We accept that everything takes forever
- We plan accordingly

The child asking "Is it time yet?" for the hundredth time isn't trying to annoy you. They literally cannot judge time's passage. They're checking if the universe has changed.

And sometimes, when they ask "Is it tomorrow yet?" at 3 AM, the kindest answer is "Yes, but tomorrow is sleeping time too."

And in the time universe of parenting, sleep is the only measurement that matters.

CHAPTER 19

The Sarcasm Shift (Around ages 8-10)

Around age 8-10, language gets weird. Really weird.

> *"Oh, GREAT, it's raining."* (Meaning: This is terrible)
> *"Sure, whatever you say."* (Meaning: I don't believe you)
> *"That was REALLY helpful."* (Meaning: You made things worse)
> *"Nice going, Einstein."* (Meaning: That was stupid)
> *"Oh, I LOVE homework."* (Meaning: I hate homework)

This is universe inversion—words meaning their opposite. And it breaks children's brains completely.

For eight years, they've been building universes where words mean what they mean. "Great" means good. "Sure" means yes. "Helpful" means it helped. "Love" means affection.

Now suddenly, tone of voice can flip the entire universe upside down. The same word can mean opposite things depending on invisible social cues they're just learning to read. It's like discovering that sometimes up is down, but only on Tuesdays, and only if someone rolls their eyes while saying it.

The Literal Years

Before sarcasm, children live in the literal universe:

Around age 3: *"Good job!"* always means praise
Around age 5: *"Nice work!"* always means approval
Around age 7: *"Great!"* always means positive
Then around age 8 hits and suddenly: *"Nice going!"* might mean *"You screwed up"*
"Brilliant!" might mean *"That was stupid"*
"Perfect!" might mean *"This is a disaster"*
"Wonderful!" might mean *"I'm dead inside"*

The betrayal is profound. Language itself has become unreliable. It's like finding out your GPS sometimes deliberately gives wrong directions for fun.

The First Encounter

Watch an eight-year-old encounter sarcasm for the first time:

Dad (after child spills milk): *"Oh wonderful, that's just PERFECT."*
Child: *"It is?"*
Dad: *"No, it's not perfect. I was being sarcastic."*
Child: *"Why did you say perfect if it's not perfect?"*

Dad: *"Because... it's sarcasm."*
Child: *"So you lied?"*
Dad: *"No, it's... it's like a joke."*
Child: *"It's not funny."*
Dad: *"It's not supposed to be funny."*
Child: *"So it's a not-funny joke?"*
Dad: *"Never mind, just clean it up."*
Child: (existential crisis face)

The child has just discovered that words can mean different things. That trusted adults say the opposite of what they mean. That language has a secret code they haven't been taught. Their universe just developed a glitch in the matrix.

The Overcorrection Phase

Once children discover sarcasm, they use it wrong. Constantly. Everywhere. It's painful.

"I LOVE homework!" (attempting sarcasm)
"Do you really?"
"No! I was being sarcastic!"
"Oh."
"I LOVE broccoli!" (trying again)
"Actually you do like broccoli."
"No! Sarcasm!"
"But you ate it yesterday happily."
"That wasn't sarcasm broccoli!"

"School is THE BEST!" (maximum sarcasm attempt)
"You seemed happy this morning."
"THAT WAS SARCASM TOO!"
"Everything can't be sarcasm."
"THAT'S SARCASTIC!"
(Everyone confused)

They understand words can mean their opposite. They don't understand when, why, or how to signal it. They're using a weapon they don't know how to aim. Casualties everywhere.

Try This: The Sarcasm Signal

Teach the components explicitly:

1. **Tone change** (demonstrate exaggerated voice)
2. **Context clues** (situation makes it obvious)
3. **Facial expression** (eye roll, smirk)
4. **Social safety** (not with teachers, grandparents)
5. **Timing** (not during serious moments)
6. **Recovery** (what to do when it fails)

Practice together: *"Let's say 'Great!' happy"* (genuine)
"Now say 'Great!' sarcastic" (tone shift)
"How did your voice change?"
"How did your face change?"
"When would each be appropriate?"
"Never? That's also valid."

You're teaching them to decode the secret signals. It's like spy training but more confusing.

The Social Disaster Zone

Early sarcasm attempts create social catastrophes:

Teacher: *"Nice project!"*
Child: (detecting tone variation) *"I know you're being sarcastic!"*
Teacher: *"I'm not. It's genuinely nice."*
Child: *"You said it weird!"*
Teacher: *"I'm sincere."*
Child: *"THAT'S WHAT SARCASTIC PEOPLE SAY!"*
Teacher: (calls parents)

They're hypervigilant for inversions, finding them everywhere, even where they don't exist. Every compliment becomes suspect. Every statement might be its opposite. Trust erodes. Paranoia grows.

The Friend Group Fracture

Sarcasm divides friend groups:

The Early Adopters: Using sarcasm by around age 8
The Literal Crew: Still processing words as meaning what they mean
The Confused Middle: Sometimes getting it, sometimes not
The Overshoots: Everything is sarcastic always

Watch a mixed group:

Early Adopter: *"Yeah, that's REALLY cool."* (sarcastic)
Literal Friend: *"Thanks!"* (genuine)
Early Adopter: (eye roll)
Literal Friend: (hurt, confused)
Overshoot: *"I LOVE EVERYTHING!"* (unclear if sarcastic)
Confused Middle: *"What's happening?"*

Friendships fracture over universe mismatches. The literal child feels constantly tricked. The sarcastic child feels constantly misunderstood. The overshoot child has lost all meaning. Nobody's having fun.

The Family Sarcasm Gap

Different family members model different language universes:

Dad: Heavy sarcasm user *("Oh great, traffic, my favorite")*
Mom: Straight talker *("The traffic is bad")*

Older sibling: Sarcasm expert *("Yeah, because sitting in cars is AMAZING")*
Younger child: Literal processor *("Why is it amazing?")*

The 9-year-old is simultaneously navigating:

- Dad saying opposite of what he means
- Mom saying what she means
- Sibling using advanced sarcasm
- Having to code-switch between them
- Developing their own style
- Trying not to cry

No wonder they're exhausted and confused. They're managing four different language operating systems simultaneously.

The Cultural Collision

Sarcasm varies by culture:

A child from a literal-language family entering a high-sarcasm environment experiences constant universe vertigo. They're not slow—they're translating between incompatible systems.

"Why did she say 'nice weather' when it's raining?"
"High-sarcasm environment."
"So she's not telling the truth?"
"No, she's being funny."
"But it's not funny."
"It's her way."
"I don't understand."
"Nobody does."

The Emotional Sarcasm Wound

Sarcasm aimed at children before they understand
it causes deep confusion:

Parent (frustrated): *"Oh you're SUCH a good listener."*
Child's literal universe: *"I'm a good listener!"*
Parent's tone: Angry
Child's confusion: *"Why is mom angry that I'm good?"*
Child's conclusion: *"Nothing makes sense anymore."*

The message splits:

- **Words say:** You're good
- **Tone says:** You're bad
- **Child concludes:** I don't understand anything
- **Also concludes:** Adults are insane

This creates anxiety around all communication. Every conversation might be a trap. Every compliment might be an insult. Every insult might be affection. It's linguistic chaos.

The Humor Bridge

Some children get humor before sarcasm:

Jokes: Setup and punchline, clear structure
Puns: Wordplay with obvious double meaning
Slapstick: Physical humor, no language tricks
Sarcasm: Invisible inversion based on tone

Understanding jokes doesn't mean they'll get sarcasm. Different universes entirely. A child who loves knock-knock jokes might be completely baffled by "Nice job, butterfingers" after dropping something.

> *"But where's the punchline?"*
> *"The sarcasm IS the punchline."*
> *"That's not how jokes work."*
> *"Sarcasm is different."*
> *"Sarcasm is broken jokes?"*
> *"Sort of, yes."*

Try This: The Sarcasm Practice

Create safe sarcasm practice:

> *"Let's play the opposite game. I'll describe our day wrong:"*
> *"We had SUCH a relaxing morning!"* (rushed to school)
> *"Breakfast was GOURMET!"* (cereal)
> *"Traffic was DELIGHTFUL!"* (terrible)
> *"Your room is SO clean!"* (disaster)
>
> **Child tries:**
> *"School was SO SHORT!"* (felt long)
> *"Homework was SUPER FUN!"* (wasn't)
> *"My teacher LOVES when I talk!"* (she doesn't)
> *"Everything makes sense!"* (nothing does)

You're building sarcasm recognition in a safe, clear context where everyone knows it's practice.

The Text Problem

Modern kids encounter sarcasm in texts before they can decode it:

"Great job" (might be genuine or sarcastic)
"Sure whatever" (definitely sarcastic but no tone cues)
"K" (is this angry? sarcastic? fine?)
"That's interesting" (OH NO WHAT DOES THIS MEAN)

They're trying to decode universe inversions without voice tone, facial expressions, or context. It's impossible. Every text becomes a mystery to solve.

"Mom texted 'fine'—is she mad?"
"Why would she be mad?"
"She used a period."
"That's punctuation."
"Angry punctuation."
"Punctuation doesn't have emotions."
"You don't understand texting."
(Parent doesn't understand texting)

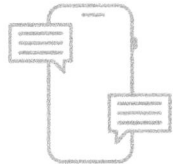

The Developmental Timeline

Around age 6-7: Literal universe only
- Words mean what they mean
- Tone confusion begins
- *"Why are you saying nice things in a mean voice?"*

Around age 8-9: Sarcasm awareness
- Recognizing it exists
- Often misidentifying it
- Attempting it badly
- Making everyone uncomfortable

Around age 10-11: Sarcasm competence
- Can identify most instances
- Can use it simply
- Still missing subtle versions
- Overshooting regularly

Around age 12-13: Sarcasm fluency
- Full recognition
- Contextual use
- Understanding when not to use
- Still using it too much

Around age 14+: Sarcasm mastery
- Multiple layers
- Social navigation
- Cultural code-switching
- Basically just sarcastic always

Around age 30+: Sarcasm exhaustion
- Can use it but tired
- Prefer straight talk
- Wonder why teenagers need to be so sarcastic
- Become parents who confuse their kids with sarcasm

What This Means

The sarcasm shift isn't just learning humor. It's discovering that language itself is unreliable, that meaning depends on invisible signals, that adults have been speaking in code.

When children struggle with sarcasm:

- They're not socially delayed
- They're rebuilding their entire language universe
- They need explicit instruction in the signals
- They need safe practice space
- They need patience when they get it wrong
- They need adults to maybe use less sarcasm

The child who takes everything literally at around age 9? They're not behind. They're operating in the universe they spent eight years building. The sarcastic universe is a complete rebuild, not an upgrade.

The child who suddenly makes everything sarcastic? They're not being rude. They're practicing a new language feature. Badly.

And maybe, just maybe, the fact that humans created a communication system where words can mean their opposite based on subtle tone shifts that vary by culture and context... maybe that's the real problem.

CHAPTER 20

When Partners Have Different Universes

Plot twist: Adults have different word universes too.

One parent says *"clean"* and means *"spotless."*
The other says *"clean"* and means *"no health hazards."*
One says *"soon"* and means *"five minutes."*
The other means *"sometime today."*
One says *"bedtime"* and means *"in bed by 8."*
The other means *"start heading up around 8-ish."*

Your child is trying to build their universe while receiving conflicting blueprints. It's like trying to learn a language where half the teachers speak French and half speak Spanish, but everyone insists they're teaching the same thing.

> *"Why can't you behave like you do for Parent B?"*
> *"Because parent B and Parent A are different games with different rules."*
> (Child more insightful than either parent realizes)

The Clean Wars

The word "clean" might cause more family conflict than any other:

Parent A's "Clean":
- No visible items on surfaces
- Everything in designated spots
- Could take a photo for magazine
- Vacuum lines visible on carpet
- Gleaming surfaces
- Beds made with hospital corners
- Smells like lemons

Parent B's "Clean":
- No actual dirt
- Path to walk through room
- Can find things if needed
- No bugs or mold
- Functional
- Bed has covers on it somewhere
- Doesn't smell bad

Child receives instruction: "Clean your room." From Parent A? Four-hour project with seventeen quality checks. From Parent B? Five-minute tidy, good enough. The child isn't confused about cleaning. They're navigating two entirely different universes labeled with the same word. They become code-switchers, checking which parent is asking before determining effort level.

The Bedtime Battle

"Bedtime" seems straightforward. It's not:

Parent A's Bedtime Universe:
- 7:30 means in bed by 7:30
- Includes: bath, teeth, story, prayers, songs
- Quiet wind-down essential
- No exceptions except illness
- Screens off one hour before
- Organic lavender essential oil diffuser activated
- White noise machine precisely calibrated

Parent B's Bedtime Universe:
- 7:30 means start heading up around then
- Teeth required, bath optional
- Story if time
- Flexible based on day
- Screens fine until pajamas
- Maybe remember to turn off hallway light
- Is that crying or singing? Either's fine

The child learns: Bedtime with Parent A and bedtime with Parent B are different events that happen to share a name. Like how both "The Office" versions are called "The Office" but one has Ricky Gervais and one has Steve Carell.

The Behavior Expectations

"Be good" from different parents:

Parent A means:
- Sit still
- Speak when spoken to
- Follow all rules exactly
- No noise
- Adult-pleasing performance
- Basically become a Victorian child

Parent B means:
- Don't break anything
- No screaming
- Generally cooperate
- Have fun
- Be yourself within reason

The child becomes a code-switcher, changing entire personalities based on which parent is present. This isn't manipulation—it's survival. They're bilingual in parental expectations.

"Why are you so good for Parent A?"
"Because Parent A has more rules and gets scarier."
(Truth bomb nobody wanted)

Try This: The Universe Summit

Sit down with your partner (without kids) and define:

- What does "clean" mean to each of you?
- What does "behave" mean?
- What does "bedtime" mean?

- What does "soon" mean?
- What does "help" mean?
- What does "in trouble" mean?

You'll discover you've been speaking different languages for years. It's like finding out your spouse has been using "love" to mean "tolerate" this whole time.

The Consequence Confusion

"If you don't stop, there will be consequences!"

Parent A's consequences:
- Immediate
- Logical connection to behavior
- Consistent every time
- Non-negotiable
- Followed through
- Remembered next time

Parent B's consequences:
- Maybe
- Eventually
- If behavior continues
- Often forgotten
- Usually negotiable
- What were we talking about?

The child learns: "Consequences" from Parent A means stop now. "Consequences" from Parent B means you have 3-4 more chances, possibly infinite if they get distracted.

Kid becomes a consequence calculator, adjusting behavior based on threat credibility assessment.

The Permission Paradox

Child: "Can I have a cookie?"

Parent A's decision tree:
- What time is it?
- When did they last eat?
- What did they eat?
- How many cookies this week?
- Did they eat vegetables?
- Is dinner soon?
- What's their behavior been like?
- Check blood sugar levels
- Consult nutritional pyramid
- Consider long-term health impacts

Parent B's decision tree:
- Are there cookies?
- Why not?
- Don't tell

The child learns to ask the right parent for different things. They're not manipulating—they're navigating different permission universes. It's strategic adaptation.

The "Ask Your Mother/Father" Loop

"Can I go to Sam's house?"
"Ask your" Parent A
"Parent A, can I go to Sam's house?"
"What did your Parent B say?"
"They said ask you."
"Well, what do you think?"
"I think yes?"
"Then why are you asking?"
"Because I need permission?"

"Ask your Parent B."
Child trapped in infinite loop.
Child goes to Sam's anyway.
(Parents blame each other)

The child is stuck in a loop between universes, neither parent wanting to contradict the other, both operating from different frameworks, the child learning that sometimes no one is actually in charge.

The Time Universe Clash

"We're leaving soon!"

Parent A: Soon = 5-10 minutes, I'm watching the clock
Parent B: Soon = 20-45 minutes, roughly
Child: Soon = ??? ERROR CANNOT COMPUTE
This is why: *"Are we leaving?"*
"Ask Parent A/Parent B."

They're not being difficult. They're trying to figure out which universe is active. It's like trying to figure out which remote controls which TV when you have seventeen remotes.

The Screen Time Schism

Parent A's Screen Rules:
- 30 minutes weekdays
- 1 hour weekends
- Educational content preferred
- No screens during meals
- Parental controls activated
- Time tracked religiously

Parent B's Screen Rules:
- Until their eyes bleed
- Whatever keeps them quiet
- YouTube is educational right?
- Screens at meals mean peace
- What are parental controls?
- Time is an illusion

Child learns to maximize screen time through strategic parent selection and careful timing of requests.

"Parent A said no iPad."
"Did they say no phone?"
"...no."
"Here's my phone."
(Loophole exploited)

The Grandparent Override

Then grandparents arrive with entirely different universes:

Parents: *"No candy before dinner"*
Grandparents: *"Here's a secret chocolate stash"*

Parents: *"Bedtime is 8 PM"*
Grandparents: *"Sleep is for the weak"*

Parents: *"They need to clean up"*
Grandparents: *"I'll do it, you play"*

Parents: *"One show only"*
Grandparents: *"Let's watch all of Disney+"*

The child's carefully constructed universes explode. Rules they thought were laws of physics are suddenly negotiable. It's like discovering gravity is optional on Tuesdays.

The Sibling Differential

"Why does HE get to...?"

Because different children might live in different parental universes:

Oldest child: Strict universe (parents learning)
Middle child: Forgotten universe (parents overwhelmed)
Youngest: Relaxed universe (parents defeated)

Same parents, same words, completely different meanings based on birth order and parental exhaustion levels.

"You let him stay up later!"
"We're too tired to fight anymore."
(Honesty that hurts)

Try This: The Family Dictionary

Create a family dictionary together:

- *"Clean"* means: [**specific** list everyone agrees on]
- *"Soon"* means: [**specific** timeframe]
- *"Bedtime routine"* includes: [**specific** steps]
- *"Good behavior"* looks like: [**specific** actions]
- *"Consequences"* means: [**specific** outcomes]

Post it. Reference it. "Check the family dictionary" becomes the neutral arbiter.

The Stress Universe Split

Under stress, parent universes diverge even more:

Parent A stressed: Rules become stricter
Parent B stressed: Rules become looser
MORNING RUSH:
Parent A's: "Everyone dressed NOW! No talking! Move!"
Parent B's: "Whatever, just get in the car, shoes optional."

The child experiences universe whiplash based on parental stress levels. They become stress detectors, adjusting behavior based on tension barometer.

The Good Cop/Bad Cop Dynamic

Without meaning to, parents often split into:

The Enforcer: Rules, consequences, structure
The Fun One: Flexibility, adventures, rule- bending

Child learns:
- **Need permission?** Ask Fun One
- **In trouble?** Appeal to Fun One
- **Fun One absent?** Negotiate with Enforcer
- **Both present?** Create confusion, exploit gap

They're not being manipulative. They're responding to the universe structure you've created.

Parent A's *"the mean one."*
Parent B's *"the pushover."*
(Both parents hurt, both right)

The Communication Breakdown

The Classic Scene:

Parent A: *"Did you tell them they could have ice cream?"*
Parent B: *"I said maybe."*
Parent A: *"They're eating ice cream."*
Parent B: *"Maybe meant yes to them."*
Parent A: *"Maybe means NO until confirmed!"*
Parent B: *"Since when?"*
Parent A: *"Since ALWAYS!"*
Child: (eating second bowl while parents argue)

The universe definitions were never aligned. The child just benefited from the confusion.

The Weekend Warrior Problem

Weekday Parent: Maintains structure, routines, rules
Weekend Parent: *"Rules? What rules? It's Saturday!"*

Child gets universe whiplash every Friday night and Sunday evening. It's like switching between military school and Burning Man every few days.

What This Means

Your child isn't confused because they're slow. They're confused because they're receiving incompatible universe blueprints from the most important people in their life.

This isn't failure—it's reality. No two adults have identical word universes because no two adults had identical childhoods building those universes.

When we recognize this:

- We stop pretending alignment exists
- We explicitly acknowledge differences
- We help children code-switch
- We reduce universe confusion
- We stop undermining each other
- We accept some chaos

The child who seems to manipulate parents against each other? They're not manipulative. They're multilingual in universe systems, translating between incompatible realities.

And that's actually a sophisticated skill that will serve them well in a world where everyone's speaking slightly different languages while pretending they're all speaking the same one.

CHAPTER 21

The Parent Reset

Children are doing something miraculous. They're building entire universes of meaning from scratch. Every word, every concept, every social rule—they're constructing it all while also learning to tie their shoes and remember not to eat paint.

When a four-year-old misunderstands your "simple" instruction, they're not failing. They're revealing the incredible complexity of human communication that we take for granted.

That meltdown over the "wrong" colored cup? They haven't built the universe where color is separate from function yet. That confusion over "yesterday" versus "last week"? Time is an abstract universe they're still mapping. That inability to "just say sorry and mean it"? The emotional universe of genuine remorse requires neural connections that won't fully develop for years.

Understanding this doesn't make parenting easier. But it makes it make sense.

The Guilt Release

Here's what you need to release:

"I should be more patient"

You're asking a brain that evolved for small tribes to navigate modern parenting with work stress, financial pressure, and no village support. Your impatience isn't failure—it's biology meeting impossible circumstances. You're doing something humans weren't designed to do alone.

"Other parents seem to handle this better"

You're seeing their highlight reel, not their 2 AM screaming matches over sock seams. Every parent is struggling with universe translation. Some just hide it better. That mom who seems perfect at pickup? She cried in her car this morning.

That dad who's always calm? He's not. We're all barely surviving and pretending otherwise.

"I'm damaging my child"

Unless you're actively abusive (and reading this book suggests you're not), you're not damaging them. You're doing universe translation without a manual. Imperfect translation isn't trauma—it's normal. Your parents did it imperfectly. Their parents did it imperfectly. Yet here we all are, functional enough to worry about being perfect.

"I should know this already"

How? Where would you have learned that "don't" processes backward in children's brains? This information didn't exist when you were raised. You're not behind—you're learning new science. You're literally the first generation of parents with access to this information.

The Repair Universe

When you mess up (and you will, daily), repair is more important than perfection:

The Rupture: You yelled because they didn't listen
The Realization: They couldn't process your rapid instructions
The Repair: *"I spoke too fast. Let me try again slowly."*

You're not admitting failure. You're modeling that:
- Mistakes happen
- Understanding improves
- Relationships repair
- Communication can retry
- Adults aren't perfect
- That's okay

Children don't need perfect parents. They need parents who repair. Perfect parents would create children who can't handle imperfection. You're actually doing them a favor by messing up regularly.

Try This: The Daily Repair

Each night, one repair:

"When I got frustrated about your shoes, I forgot you can't process 'don't.' Tomorrow I'll say 'walking feet' instead."

With

When I got frustrated about your shoes, I used confusing words. Tomorrow instead of 'don't run,' I'll say 'walking feet."

Small. Specific. Forward-looking. You're teaching them that relationships include rupture AND repair. That's a universe worth building.

The Energy Accounting

Your universe-translation capacity is finite:

Morning: 100% capacity

- Can slow down
- Can translate abstracts to concrete
- Can stay calm
- Might even smile

After work: 50% capacity
- Shorter sentences needed
- Less translation available
- Patience depleted
- Fake smile sometimes

Bedtime: 10% capacity
- Single words only
- No complex instructions
- Survival mode
- What smile?

After bedtime: -20% capacity
- Cannot form words
- Children must self-regulate
- Or not, whatever

This isn't failure. It's energy physics. Plan accordingly:
- Complex conversations in morning
- Simple routines for evening
- Survival mode for bedtime
- Complete surrender after 8 PM

The Comparison Trap

"That mom speaks so calmly to her kids." That mom might:

- Have more support
- Be medicated for anxiety
- Have easier temperament children
- Be performing for public
- Go home and collapse
- Have different capacity
- Actually be on her phone while kids destroy things

Comparing your inside to their outside is universe mismatch. You're not seeing their full reality. You're seeing their parking lot performance.

The Generation Healing Myth

"I need to break the cycle!" Maybe. Or maybe:

- Your parents did their best with zero information
- You're doing your best with some information
- Your kids will do their best with more information
- Evolution, not revolution
- Progress, not perfection

You don't need to be perfect to be better. Small improvements compound across generations. Your kids will raise their kids differently than you're raising up yours. That's progress.

The Success Redefinition

Success isn't:
- Perfect behavior
- Early milestones
- Constant happiness
- No meltdowns
- Pinterest-worthy crafts
- Organic everything
- Screen-free childhood
- Bilingual by three

Success is:
- Everyone survived today
- One universe connection made
- Slightly better than yesterday
- Repair after rupture
- Still trying
- Nobody's in jail
- Kids are fed (cereal counts)
- You haven't run away (yet)

Lower the bar to where you and your child can succeed, then celebrate that success.

Try This: The Success Journal

Each day, write one tiny success:

- *"Used positive instruction instead of 'don't'"*
- *"Recognized universe collapse before meltdown"*
- *"Slowed down for one instruction"*
- *"Repaired after yelling"*
- *"Fed children food"*
- *"Everyone has clothes on"*
- *"We're all alive"*

Not perfection. Progress. Sometimes just survival.

The Overwhelm Protocol

When you're drowning in universe translation:

STEP 1: Lower all expectations
- Cereal for dinner is fine
- Screens are survival tools
- Matching socks are optional
- Vegetables are aspirational
- Bedtime is negotiable

STEP 2: Simplify to concrete
- No abstract instructions
- Only physical, visible tasks
- Single steps only

STEP 3: Borrow universes
- Let school handle complex learning
- Let grandparents take over
- Let some chaos reign

STEP 4: Rest without guilt
- You're not lazy
- You're recharging translation capacity
- Empty battery can't translate
- Full battery also struggles but less

The Milestone Trap

"They should be [insert milestone] by now!"

According to whom? Milestones are averages, not laws. Your child might be:

- Building universes in different order
- Focusing on different universes
- Needing more repetitions
- Following their own blueprint
- Completely normal
- Also completely unique

The child "behind" in pronouns might be "ahead" in spatial reasoning. Universe construction isn't a race. It's not even a journey. It's more like a chaotic explosion in multiple directions simultaneously.

The Partner Reality

When partners have different universes (Chapter 20), someone needs to translate. Usually you. Always you.

Instead of: *"You're too strict/lenient!"*
Try: *"We have different clean universes. How do we help kid navigate both?"*

Instead of: *"You always undermine me!"*
Try: *"Kid is getting confused by our different bedtime universes. Let's clarify."*

You're not fighting. You're recognizing you speak different languages. And somehow you're supposed to teach a third person who speaks neither.

The Self-Compassion Mandate

You're doing impossible work:

- Translating between universes
- Without training
- With depleted resources
- While also working
- And maintaining a household
- And pretending to be fine

Every day you translate between universes, you're doing neurological interpretation work that no generation before you understood.

You're not failing when it's hard. You're succeeding every time you try.

The Future Universe

Your child will eventually build all their universes. They will understand abstracts, process "don't," grasp time, navigate sarcasm. It will happen.

Not on your timeline. Not on the chart's timeline. On their brain's timeline.

Your job isn't to speed it up. It's to translate while they build. To be the bridge between their universe and the adult world. To stay somewhat sane while doing it.

What This Means

The parent reset isn't about becoming different. It's about understanding what's actually happening:

- You're doing impossible work
- Without training
- With depleted resources
- And still succeeding
- Even when it doesn't feel like it
- Especially when it doesn't feel like it

Every time you slow down to translate, every time you recognize universe collision, every time you repair after rupture—you're doing the work.

It's exhausting. It's relentless. It's largely thankless.

It's also miraculous. You're helping a small human build their entire understanding of reality, one word at a time, one concept at a time, one exhausting day at a time.

And someday, probably when they have their own children, they'll understand what you did. They'll call you at 2 AM when their child is melting down about the wrong cup, and they'll say, "How did you do this?"

And you'll say, "Badly. But with love." And that will be the truth.

And it will be enough.

CHAPTER 22

Different Architects, Different Blueprints

Remember everything I've described about how children build word universes? Now I need to tell you something important: I've been describing the most common blueprint. But some children—maybe yours—are working from different architectural plans entirely.

This isn't a consolation chapter. It's not about "disorders" or "delays" or "problems." It's recognition that human brains are diverse, that different doesn't mean broken, and that some of the most innovative minds in history built their universes in completely unique ways.

Your child who lines up cars for hours? Who knows every dinosaur fact but can't remember to say hello? Who feels socks like sandpaper? They're not building wrong. They're building differently.

The Timeline Variations

Here's what typical development charts won't tell you: "Typical" is a statistical average, not a requirement. It's like saying the "typical" height is 5'9". That doesn't make 5'2" or 6'4" wrong. It makes them variations.

Some children build universes in unexpected orders:

The Specialist Builder: Masters complex universes while missing "simple" ones
- Knows every Pokemon evolution around age 4
- Can't understand "friend" around age 8
- Memorizes subway systems
- Can't grasp "soon"
- Recites entire movies
- Can't answer "how was your day?"
- Builds deep, narrow universes instead of broad, shallow ones

This isn't a deficit with advanced patches. It's a completely different architecture. Their brain prioritizes different universes, builds in different sequences, creates different connections.

They're not behind with islands of genius. They're using an entirely different blueprint.

The Sensory Intensity Architects

Some children experience sensory input at different volumes than typical:

The High-Volume Processor:
- Fluorescent lights are painful
- Seams in socks are unbearable
- Can hear electricity humming
- Smells others don't notice
- Touch registers intensely
- Tags are torture devices
- Cucumber has a sound
- Can taste the difference between water brands

When this child melts down in Target, they're not spoiled. Their sensory universes are experiencing input at 10x volume. Imagine every sound amplified, every light brightened, every touch intensified, every smell overwhelming. That's their normal.

"Why are you crying?"
"The lights are screaming."
"Lights don't scream."
"THEY DO TO ME!"
(Both are right)

The Low-Volume Processor:
- Doesn't notice they're hurt
- Seems not to hear you
- Needs intense input to register
- Seeks crash, squeeze, pressure
- May seem "in their own world"
- Loves tight spaces
- Might not notice hunger/thirst
- Temperature doesn't register normally

278 Why Won't You Listen?

They're not ignoring you. Their sensory universes require more input to register. What seems like defiance might be genuinely not processing regular-volume input. You're broadcasting on AM, they're receiving on FM.

Try This: The Sensory Map

Without judgment, map your child's sensory preferences:

- What do they avoid? (might be too intense)
- What do they seek? (might need more input)
- When do they focus best? (optimal sensory state)
- What helps them calm? (sensory regulation)
- What causes instant meltdown? (sensory overload)

This isn't diagnosis. It's recognition of their specific blueprint. Like knowing someone needs glasses isn't a diagnosis, it's an observation.

The Movement Processors

Some brains build universes through movement:

The Kinesthetic Builder:
- Can't sit still to learn
- Remembers better while walking
- Needs to touch everything
- Thinks better while moving
- May seem "hyperactive"
- Fidgets to focus
- Learns through doing, not watching
- Body is their thinking tool

This isn't excess energy or poor control. Their brain appears to construct understanding through movement. Asking them to sit still to learn is like asking you to learn while holding your breath.

"Sit still and pay attention!"
"I AM paying attention!"
"You're bouncing!"
"That's HOW I pay attention!"
(Child is right)

Schools often punish these builders, removing recess (movement) as consequence for not sitting still (impossible for them). It's like punishing someone for needing glasses by taking away their glasses.

The Pattern Masters

Some children see patterns others miss:

The System Builder:
- Notices if one book is out of order
- Remembers exact sequences
- Distressed by routine changes
- Sees patterns in everything
- May line things up constantly
- Counts everything
- Notices when things move
- Remembers where everything was

This isn't rigidity or control issues. Their brain is constantly pattern-mapping, finding systems, creating order. What looks like "obsessive" behavior is actually universe construction at a different resolution.

"Why are you lining up cars AGAIN?"
"They have a system."
"What system?"
"Color gradient from light to dark with size subcategorization."
"You're four."
"So?"

These children might struggle with:
- Flexibility (patterns shouldn't change)
- Transitions (breaking current pattern)
- Social situations (humans are unpredictable)
- "About" or "around" (needs exactness)

But they excel at:
- Memory for details
- Spotting errors
- Creating systems
- Deep knowledge acquisition
- Quality control
- Future engineering careers

The Emotional Intensity Architects

Some children experience emotions at different intensities:

The Deep Feelers:
- Joy is ecstasy
- Disappointment is devastation
- Anger is rage
- Love is overwhelming
- Sadness is despair
- Excitement is explosion
- Everything is intense
- No medium settings

They're not dramatic or manipulative. Their emotional universes operate at higher intensity. Asking them to "calm down" is like asking someone to make their eyes less blue.

"It's just a small disappointment."
"THERE'S NO SUCH THING AS SMALL!"
(In their universe, this is true)

These children need:
- Recognition that their feelings are real
- Tools for intensity management (not suppression)
- Time to process big emotions
- Adults who don't minimize their experience
- Understanding that they're not choosing this

The Asynchronous Developers

Some children might build universes at wildly different rates:

The Scattered Timeline:
- Reading at college level, around age 7
- Can't tie shoes, around age 10
- Understands quantum physics concepts
- Can't remember to brush teeth
- Discusses philosophy
- Melts down over sandwich cutting
- Solves complex problems
- Can't find their backpack that they're wearing

This isn't laziness or selective competence. Different brain regions are developing at different rates. They're not choosing to be "gifted" in some areas and "delayed" in others. Their brain is building universes on its own timeline.

"How can you understand calculus but not remember your lunch?"
"Different brain departments."
"That's not how brains work."
"Mine does."

The Processing Speed Variations

Some children process at different speeds:

The Slow, Deep Processor:
- Takes longer to respond
- Needs time to think
- Produces thoughtful answers
- May seem "slow"
- Often highly intelligent
- Quality over speed
- Hates being rushed
- Processing, not ignoring

They're not delayed. They're thorough. Their brain won't produce an answer until it's fully formed. Rushing them produces anxiety, not faster processing.

"Answer the question!"
"I'm building the answer."
"Build faster!"
"That breaks the answer."

The Rapid Surface Processor:
- Answers immediately
- May miss depth
- Seems impulsive
- Quick but sometimes wrong

- Needs help slowing down
- Quantity over quality
- Says things without thinking
- Processes while speaking

They're not careless. Their brain might prioritizes speed over accuracy. They need help building pauses, checking work, second thoughts.

The Social Universe Variations

Some children build social universes differently:

The Parallel Player:
- Prefers alongside, not interactive play
- Happy alone
- Overwhelmed by group dynamics
- May have few but deep friendships
- Thinks of others differently
- Enjoys watching more than joining
- Social energy depletes quickly
- Not lonely, just different

This isn't antisocial or unfriendly. Their social universe has different physics. Where others gain energy from interaction, they spend it. Where others fear alone, they recharge.

"Go play with the others!"
"I am playing with them."
"You're sitting alone."
"We're playing separately together."
(This is valid play)

The Communication Builders

Some children may communicate differently:

The Alternative Communicators:
- May speak late or not at all
- Use gestures, pictures, or devices
- Understand more than they express
- May echo others' speech
- Build language differently
- Might speak in scripts
- Could lose speech when stressed
- Communication isn't just talking

Communication difference isn't intelligence difference. Some of the world's greatest minds communicate alternatively.

"Use your words!"
"I am! Just not mouth words."

Supporting Different Blueprints

If your child's blueprint differs from typical:

Recognize Strengths:
- What comes easily?
- What do they love?
- Where do they shine?
- What patterns do you see?
- What's their superpower?

Accommodate Differences:

- Sensory needs aren't preferences
- Movement needs aren't choices
- Processing speed isn't changeable
- Intensity isn't wrong
- Different isn't less

Build Bridges:

- Between their universe and typical expectations
- Between their strengths and challenges
- Between home and school
- Between their needs and world's demands
- Between different and accepted

Advocate Fiercely:

- Their different blueprint is valid
- They deserve accommodation
- Their way of building universes matters
- They're not broken
- They're not wrong
- They're not less
- They're different

Try This: The Blueprint Celebration

Write down five things that make your child's blueprint unique:

1. What they notice that others miss
2. How they process differently
3. What they might need that others don't
4. What comes easily that's hard for others
5. Their unique universe-building style

This isn't "making excuses" or "lowering expectations." It's recognizing the architect they are, not lamenting the architect they're not.

What This Means

Different blueprints aren't deficits. They're variations. Your child with sensory intensity isn't broken—they may be high-definition in a standard-definition world. Your movement-needing child isn't hyperactive—they may be kinesthetic in a sedentary system. Your pattern-focused child isn't rigid—they may be systematic in a chaotic environment.

The history of human innovation is written by different architects:

- Einstein built universes differently (allegedly couldn't tie shoes)
- Mozart processed sound differently
- Temple Grandin thinks in pictures
- Many innovators were "different" children
- Most changed the world because of, not despite, their differences

When we recognize different blueprints:

- We stop trying to rebuild our children
- We start accommodating their architecture
- We celebrate their unique construction
- We help them navigate a typical-blueprint world
- We change the world to include them

Your different architect isn't building wrong. They're building differently. And different architects create the innovations that change the world.

The child who knows every dinosaur but can't make friends? Future paleontologist. The child who feels everything too intensely? They could be the next artist. The child who needs to move? They could be the next athlete or dancer. The child who sees patterns everywhere. They could be the next mathematician.

They're not broken. They're specialized.

And maybe, just maybe, the world needs their specific blueprint exactly as it is.

PART VII

Your Toolkit

CHAPTER 23

The Discovery Exercises

Here are ways to explore the word universes—yours and theirs. These aren't tests. They're revelations. They're conversations. They're bridges between the universes you've built and the ones your child is constructing.

After everything we've explored together—the icebergs, the "don't" processing, the midnight water phenomenon, the why spirals— these exercises are your practical toolkit. Your universe- building equipment. Your sanity preservation kit.

Exercise 1: The Word Archaeology

Pick a word you use often with your child. Let's say "careful." Now dig deep:

Your Archaeological Layers:

- When did you first understand this word?
- Who taught it to you?
- What experiences built its meaning?
- What physical sensations connect to it?
- What emotions does it carry?
- How many contexts can you use it in?
- What disasters happened when you weren't careful?

Write it all down. You'll discover *"careful"* contains:

- Physical caution (don't fall)
- Emotional protection (careful with feelings)
- Object preservation (careful with toys)
- Future thinking (careful planning)
- Social awareness (careful with words)
- That time you broke grandma's vase
- Your mother's worried voice
- The scar from not being careful

Now ask your child: *"What does careful mean?"* They might say:

- *"Don't break it"*
- *"Go slow"*
- *"Mommy's worried voice"*
- *"That thing you say a lot"*
- *"I don't know but you say it when your eye twitches"*

The gap between your archaeology and their definition? That's the universe they haven't built yet. And now you know exactly what needs construction.

Try This: The Weekly Word

Each week, pick one common word. Do the archaeology. Map the gap. Then intentionally build:

Monday:
"Careful means protecting things from breaking"
Tuesday:
"Careful with our words means not hurting feelings"
Wednesday: "
Careful walking means watching where we step"
Thursday:
"Remember when you weren't careful with the juice?"
Friday:
Everyone's covered in juice again, abandon careful lessons

You're consciously constructing universe connections. One sticky floor at a time.

Exercise 2: The Translation Game

For one day, translate yourself:

Every abstract instruction gets a concrete follow-up:

"Be patient (that means wait quietly) while I finish"
"I'm overwhelmed (my brain feels too full and fuzzy)"
"We'll go after lunch (when we're done eating the sandwiches)"
"Soon (after two Bluey episodes)"
"Clean up (toys in box, books on shelf, clothes in hamper, crayons... somewhere)"

The Advanced Version:

Have your child translate you back:

You: *"Clean up please"*
Child: *"You mean put toys in the box?"*
You: *"Yes! And books on shelf"*
Child: *"And dirty clothes in hamper?"*
You: *"Exactly!"*
Child: *"What about the slime I made?"*
You: *"The what?"*
Child: *"Nothing"*

They're showing you their universe. You're confirming or correcting. Both of you are building. And finding hidden slime.

Exercise 3: The Reverse Dictionary

*Ask your child to explain common words to an alien
who's never been to Earth:*

"What is 'sharing'?"
"What is 'tomorrow'?"
"What is 'friend'?"
"What is 'clean'?"
"What is 'sorry'?"
"What is 'bedtime'?"

Their explanations reveal exactly which parts of the universe they've constructed:

"Sharing is when someone takes your toys but mom says it's okay"
"Tomorrow is not now but also not yesterday"
"Friend is someone who plays what I want"
"Clean is when mom stops yelling"
"Sorry is the magic word that fixes angry"
"Bedtime is when fun stops"

Each answer is a universe map. Now you know where to build bridges.

Exercise 4: The Confusion Collection

Keep a notebook for a week. Every time your child seems confused by an instruction or word, write it down. Don't judge it, just collect it.

Monday:
- Confused by "put shoes by door" (put them behind door)
- Confused by "be nice" (said hi then hit)
- Confused by "five minutes" (asked every 30 seconds)
- Confused by existence of Monday

Tuesday:
- Confused by "gentle" (pat really hard)
- Confused by "inside voice" (whispered too quiet)
- Confused by "share" (gave everything away then cried)
- Still confused by Monday

At week's end, you'll have a map of universes still under construction.

Exercise 5: The Memory Bridge

When teaching a new abstract concept, anchor it to their memory:

> *"Remember when you fell off your bike? That scary feeling before you knew if you were hurt? That's called 'shock'"*
>
> *"Remember when the ice cream truck left before we got there? That sad-mad feeling? That's 'disappointment'"*
>
> *"Remember when you helped Sam when he dropped his crayons? That warm feeling after? That's 'pride'"*
>
> *"Remember when you ate that whole cake? That sick feeling? That's 'consequences'"*
>
> **The Reverse Memory Bridge:**
>
> Have them find memories:
>
> **You:** *"Tell me about a time you felt frustrated"*
> **Child:** *"When?"*
> **You:** *"When you wanted something but couldn't have it"*
> **Child:** *"Like when the toy was too high?"*
> **You:** *"Yes! That feeling is frustration"*
> **Child:** *"I feel frustration about vegetables"*

Now "frustrated" has memory anchors. Multiple, vegetable-related anchors.

Exercise 6: The Daily Universe Check

Before bed, ask: "What new universe did we build today?"

Make it concrete:

- *"You learned that 'anxious' is butterflies in tummy"*
- *"You discovered 'patient' at doctor is different from patient for cookies"*
- *"You found out 'behind' changes when people turn around"*
- *"You learned mom has a limit and we found it"*

The Universe Journal:

Keep a simple journal:

Date: March 15
New Universe: *"Consequence"*
How we built it: Toy broke when thrown, couldn't play with it
Connection made: Actions lead to results we might not like
Child's response: *"Consequences are stupid"*
Parent's response: *"Yes"*

You're documenting universe construction. In a year, you'll be amazed at the architecture. Or traumatized. Both valid.

Exercise 7: The Confusion Signal

Teach children to signal when the universe is missing:

The Basic Signals:
- *"What does that mean?"*
- *"Can you show me?"*
- *"I don't understand"*
- *"Is that like [something they know]?"*
- *"My brain doesn't have that word"*
- *"Are you speaking English?"*

The Advanced Signals:
- *"Which kind of clean?"*
- *"How long is soon?"*
- *"Nice like quiet or nice like sharing?"*
- *"Where exactly is 'by'?"*
- *"Is this real or sarcasm?"*
- *"Can you use normal words?"*

You're teaching them to identify and communicate universe gaps. It's self-advocacy training.

Exercise 8: The Both/And Bridge

For children struggling with opposing truths:

"You love your sister AND you're mad at her"
"You want to go to school AND you want to stay home"
"You're excited AND scared"
"You're hungry AND nothing sounds good"
"You're tired AND can't sleep"
"You hate me AND need me"

The Feeling Weather Report:

"What's your weather today?"
- Sunny (happy)
- Cloudy (sad)
- Stormy (angry)
- Partly cloudy (mixed)
- Tornado warning (watch out)
- Category 5 hurricane (evacuate)

"Can weather be sunny and rainy?"
"Yes! Rainbow weather!"
"Feelings can be mixed too"
"My feelings are a tornado rainbow"
"That's... actually perfect"

Exercise 9: The Success Celebration

Celebrate universe construction:

"You just figured out what 'between' means!"
"You used 'frustrated' correctly!"
"You remembered that 'soon' is longer than 'minute'!"
"You didn't hit when you were angry!"
"You understood sarcasm!"
"You realized I was at my limit!"

Make invisible mental construction visible and celebrated. Like participation trophies but for actual growth.

Exercise 10: The Parent Translation Check

This one's for you. Check your own translations:

Are you:
- Using abstract language and expecting concrete results?
- Speaking at adult speed to a child processor?
- Forgetting the "don't" problem?
- Expecting generalization across contexts?
- Assuming shared definitions with your partner?
- Building universes or just expecting them to exist?

Every frustration is a translation opportunity. Every meltdown is data. Every "why won't you listen?" is really "what universe is missing?"

The Family Meeting Exercise

Once a month, have a universe check:

- What words are confusing?
- What rules need clarifying?
- What universes are under construction?
- What bridges need building?

Make it fun. Make it safe. Make it brief. Make it include snacks.

The Final Exercise: The Compassion Practice

Every night, remind yourself:

- They're not defying you
- They're building universes from scratch
- You're doing impossible translation work
- Everyone's doing their best
- Tomorrow is another chance
- Bedtime exists
- This too shall pass

You're not just teaching words. You're architecting understanding. And that's exhausting. And miraculous. And worth it.

Even when it doesn't feel worth it. Especially then.

The Universe You've Built

So here we are. At the end of this journey through word universes, comprehension illusions, and midnight water meltdowns. You now know why your child touched the thing immediately after you said "don't touch." You understand the blue cup crisis. You see the "why" spiral for what it is—universe construction, not torture (though it's also torture).

You've discovered that:
- Words are icebergs
- *"Don't"* processes backward
- Pronouns are shape-shifters
- Time is meaningless to small humans
- Sarcasm breaks brains
- Digital natives think undo should exist for cookies
- Partners speak different languages
- Some children build differently
- Everyone's confused
- Nobody really knows what they're doing

But here's what matters: You're not failing. You're translating between universes. Your child isn't defying you. They're showing you exactly which universes they've built and which are still under construction.

That frustration you feel when they don't follow "simple" instructions? Valid. Their confusion when words mean different things in different places? Also valid. You're both right. You're both struggling. You're both doing universe construction without a manual.

The Truth About Listening

Your child does listen. They're listening so hard their little brains are smoking from the effort. They're just processing what they hear through incomplete universes, at slower speeds, with different physics than you expect.

> When you understand this, everything changes:
> - Your instructions become clearer
> - Your patience increases (slightly)
> - Your expectations adjust
> - Your compassion grows

The Gift of Understanding

You've given yourself and your child an incredible gift—the gift of understanding what's actually happening. Not judgment. Not frustration. Not "why won't you listen?" But "ah, that universe doesn't exist yet."

This understanding doesn't make parenting easier. But it makes it make sense. And sometimes, making sense is enough to get us through the day.

The Future Universes

Your child will build all their universes. Eventually. They'll understand abstracts, process "don't," grasp time, navigate sarcasm, repair relationships, and maybe even understand why you watch the news (but probably not).

They'll build universes you never imagined. Digital universes. Social universes. Future universes we can't conceive. They're not just learning your language—they're creating new ones.

And someday, probably around 2 AM when their own child is melting down about the wrong cup, they'll call you. And they'll say the words every parent waits to hear: *"How did you do this?"*

And you'll tell them the truth:

> *"I had no idea what I was doing. But I kept showing up. I kept translating. I kept building bridges. I messed up constantly. I repaired when I could. And somehow, we built enough universes together that you survived."*

The Final Universe

The most important universe you're building isn't made of words. It's made of moments. The moment you slow down to translate. The moment you recognize universe collapse instead of defiance. The moment you repair instead of punish. The moment you see your different architect as magnificent instead of difficult.

These moments build the universe of unconditional love. Of being seen. Of being understood. Of being accepted even when the universes don't align.

That's the universe that matters. That's the universe that lasts. That's the universe your child will remember.

Not that you were perfect. But that you tried to understand. Not that you never lost patience. But that you came back.

Not that you had all the answers. But that you kept showing up for the questions. All 109,500 of them per year.

The Last Word (Almost)

Your four-year-old who can't process "don't"? They're not broken. They're perfectly four.

Your eight-year-old drowning in sarcasm confusion? They're not behind. They're rebuilding their entire language universe.

Your differently-wired child building universes in unique order? They're not wrong. They're revolutionary.

You, exhausted parent trying to translate between universes while maintaining sanity? You're not failing. You're doing holy work.

You're building bridges between universes. You're helping small humans construct reality. You're creating understanding where confusion reigns.

That's not just parenting. That's universe architecture. That's meaning-making. That's love in action.

Even when it's hard. Especially when it's hard. Always when it's 2 AM and someone needs water in the blue cup.

The Actual Last Word

They do listen.

You're doing better than you think. Everyone's universes are under construction. And that's okay.

That's childhood. That's parenthood. That's the beautiful, maddening, exhausting, miraculous work of helping small humans build their universes, one word at a time, one concept at a time, one patient (or impatient) moment at a time.

Welcome to the gap. You're not alone here.

We're all just trying to understand each other across the universe divide.

And sometimes, understanding that nobody fully understands is the most comforting understanding of all.

Now go. Your child is probably doing something that requires you to say "don't" even though you now know it won't work.

Use "walking feet" instead. You've got this.

Sort of.

Good enough.

That's all any of us have.

PRACTICAL APPENDIX

Quick Translation Guide

*For when you need immediate universe translation
in the thick of parenting*

Common Daily Instructions

Instead of: *"Don't run!"*
Try: *"Walking feet"* or *"Slow body"*

Instead of: *"Be careful!"*
Try: *"Two hands on your cup"* or *"Watch where your feet go"*
or *"Move slowly"*

Instead of: *"Stop that!"*
Try: *"Hands down"* or *"Feet on floor"* or [specific action they
should do]

Instead of: *"Clean your room"*
Try: *"Toys in the bin, books on shelf, clothes in hamper"*

Instead of: *"Behave yourself"*
Try: *"Quiet voice, gentle hands, walking feet"*

Instead of: *"Pay attention"*
Try: *"Eyes on me"* or *"Listen to my words"*

Abstract to Concrete Translations

Instead of: *"Be responsible"*
Try: *"Put your backpack by the door when you come home"*

Instead of: *"Be nice to your sister"*
Try: *"Use gentle touches"* or *"Share one toy with her"*

Instead of: *"Show respect"*
Try: *"Look at people when they talk"* or *"Say please and thank you"*

Instead of: *"Be patient"*
Try: *"Wait until I count to ten"* or *"Wait until this song ends"*

Instead of: *"Cooperate"*
Try: *"We do this together"* or *"Your turn to help"*

Time Translations

Instead of: *"In a minute"*
Try: *"After I finish this"* [show what you're doing]

Instead of: *"Soon"*
Try: *"After lunch"* or *"When Dad comes home"*

Instead of: *"Later"*
Try: *"After your nap"* or *"After two TV shows"*

Instead of: *"We're leaving in 20 minutes"*
Try: *"After one more episode"* or *"When the timer beeps"*

Emotional Moment Translations

Instead of: *"Calm down!"*
Try: *"Take three deep breaths with me"* or *"Let's count to ten"*

Instead of: *"Use your words"*
Try: *"Tell me: are you mad or sad?"* or *"Point to what you want"*

Instead of: *"That's not appropriate"*
Try: *"We don't hit. Use gentle touches"* or *"Inside voice here"*

Instead of: *"Control yourself"*
Try: *"Hands in your pockets"* or *"Squeeze this pillow"*

Restaurant/Public Translations

Instead of: *"Behave in the restaurant"*
Try: *"Sit in your chair, quiet voice, food stays on plate"*

Instead of: *"Use your manners"*
Try: *"Say please to the waiter"* or *"Napkin on your lap"*

Instead of: *"Be good at the store"*
Try: *"Hold the cart, walking feet, hands to yourself"*

Bedtime Translations

Instead of: *"Get ready for bed"*
Try: *"Pajamas on, teeth brushed, pick one book"*

Instead of: *"Settle down"*
Try: *"Lay your head on the pillow"* or *"Close your eyes"*

Instead of: *"Go to sleep"*
Try: *"Rest your body, close your eyes, stay in bed"*

Emergency/Safety Translations

For immediate danger, skip "don't" entirely

Instead of: *"Don't touch the stove!"*
Try: *"STOP!"* or *"Hands back!"* or *"Hot! Danger!"*

Instead of: *"Don't run into the street!"*
Try: *"FREEZE!"* or *"STOP body!"*

Key Translation Principles

1. Make it physical: Turn abstract concepts into concrete actions

2. Be specific: Say exactly what TO do, not what NOT to do

3. Use visuals: Point, demonstrate, or show

4. Keep it short: Two-word instructions work best under age 5

5. One step at a time: Break complex tasks into single actions

Note: Every child's universe develops differently.
These translations are starting points.

A Note on this Book and Resource Information

This book offers one framework for understanding why children seem not to listen. The "universe" metaphor helps explain real developmental phenomena in practical terms. When I describe children asking "let's say 300 questions a day," I'm helping you grasp the relentless nature of their curiosity, not citing research.

The core insights—that children process language differently than adults, that abstract concepts develop slowly, that context dramatically affects behavior—reflect established developmental principles. My interpretation through "universe-building" is one way to make sense of your daily experience.

For Those Who Want to Dig Deeper

The science behind these insights isn't just academic theory—it's fascinating research that explains why bedtime takes two hours and why your child touched the stove immediately after you said "don't." I've translated the key studies into plain English with practical applications.

You'll find a few examples in the *Research Notes* section at the back of this book—enough to show that this isn't made-up parent theory but accessible interpretations of real developmental science. The complete *Professional Resource Guide*, containing over 28 research summaries, is available as a free download at **www.recognitionpress.com**. Therapists, educators, and other professionals may find this expanded guide particularly useful, as it includes academic citations and clinical applications for using these concepts in practice.

Fair warning: You might find yourself reading about pronoun development at 2 AM and finding it weirdly comforting to know that when your child says "You want cookie" instead of "I want cookie," they're demonstrating a phenomenon that researchers have been studying for decades. You're not alone in this confusion. Science is confused too, just with fancier words.

For Parents Seeking Support

If your child's development concerns you, please consult:

- Your pediatrician for developmental screening
- Early intervention services (available free in most areas for children under 3)
- Your school district's child find program (free evaluation for children 3+)
- A developmental psychologist or neuropsychologist for comprehensive evaluation

For Additional Perspectives

- "How to Talk So Kids Will Listen" (Faber & Mazlish)
- "The Whole-Brain Child" (Siegel & Bryson)
- "The Explosive Child" (Greene)

Online Resources

- zerotothree.org (development basics)
- developingchild.harvard.edu (brain science made accessible)
- understood.org (learning differences)

Final Note

Every child builds their understanding differently. Every parent translates imperfectly. This book normalizes both realities. If it helps you respond with more patience tomorrow or understand why at 2 AM your child is melting down over the wrong cup, it worked.

The Research Notes that follow aren't required reading—the book stands completely on its own. But if you're a professional needing citations, a parent who loves understanding the "why," or someone hiding from bedtime duties, you might find them surprisingly readable.

Because it turns out that understanding the science of why your four-year-old can't process "don't" is oddly comforting at 2 AM when they're doing exactly what you just told them not to do.

Again.

Research Notes:
Selected Examples

The following are sample entries from the complete
Professional Resource Guide, *which contains summaries of over*
28 key studies supporting the concepts in this book. The full guide is
available as a free download at **www.recognitionpress.com.**

The "Don't" Processing Phenomenon

Munakata, Y., et al. (2011). A unified framework for inhibitory control. *Trends in Cognitive Sciences*

What the Research Says: This research explains why children do things immediately after being told "don't." The action pathway in the brain activates before the inhibition pathway can stop it. It's not defiance—it's neurological sequencing.

Why It Matters for the Book: This is the scientific validation for Chapter 12's revelation about "don't" processing backward. The child who touches something immediately after "don't touch" isn't defying you—their brain processed "touch" before "don't."

Practical Applications:

- **In behavior modification:** Always phrase instructions positively. "Walking feet" instead of "don't run." You're speaking directly to the action pathway.

- **At home:** Every "don't" is fighting your child's neurology. Positive instructions work with their brain instead of against it.

- **For safety planning:** In true emergencies, use "STOP!" or "FREEZE!"—positive commands for stillness, not negated actions.

The Comprehension Illusion

Carey, S. (2009). *The origin of concepts.*

What the Research Says: Carey's groundbreaking work shows that children don't just learn words—they build entire conceptual systems. Abstract concepts like "time," "number," and "mind" require years of cognitive development and can't be taught through definition alone.

Why It Matters for the Book: This is the scientific foundation for Chapter 8's "Abstraction Ladder." When you tell a four-year-old to "be responsible," you're using a concept that requires cognitive architecture they haven't built yet. Carey explains why they literally cannot understand what you're asking.

Practical Applications:

- **In behavioral interventions:** Replace abstract expectations with concrete actions. Not "be good" but "hands to yourself, walking feet, quiet voice."

- **At home:** Build abstract concepts gradually through concrete experiences. "Patience" starts with "waiting for the timer to beep."

- **For curriculum design:** Sequence learning from concrete to abstract, allowing years for concept building, not weeks.

Individual Differences and Different Blueprints

Pellicano, E., & den Houting, J. (2022). Annual Research Review: Shifting from 'normal science' to neurodiversity.

What the Research Says: This paradigm-shifting review argues for understanding neurological differences as variations rather than deficits. Different cognitive styles bring different strengths and challenges, all valuable for human diversity.

Why It Matters for the Book: This is the scientific foundation for Chapter 22's celebration of different architects. The child building universes in unusual order isn't doing it wrong—they're contributing to human cognitive diversity.

Practical Applications:

- **In assessment:** Identify strengths alongside challenges. Different cognitive architecture brings unique abilities.

- **At home:** Your "difficult" child might be showing traits that lead to innovation in adulthood. Today's challenge is tomorrow's superpower.

- **For education:** Accommodate different learning styles rather than forcing conformity. Diversity in thinking benefits everyone.

Executive Function and Universe Collapse

Diamond, A. (2013). Executive functions. *Annual Review of Psychology*

What the Research Says: Diamond's comprehensive review shows that executive functions (working memory, inhibitory control, cognitive flexibility) develop slowly through childhood and aren't fully mature until the mid-20s. Young children literally lack the brain architecture for consistent self-control.

Why It Matters for the Book: This is the neuroscience behind Chapter 12's "Don't Processing Problem" and Chapter 10's "universe collapse." When a tired, hungry child can't follow simple instructions, it's not defiance—their executive function is depleted and cannot operate.

Practical Applications:

- **In behavior management:** Recognize that inhibitory control is limited and depletes throughout the day. Expect less, not more, as children tire.

- **At home:** Morning compliance will always be better than evening. Plan accordingly— save complex tasks for when executive function is fresh.

- **For classroom management:** After lunch, after recess, end of day—these are executive function danger zones. Adjust expectations.

These examples represent the type of accessible, practical research translations available in the complete guide. Each entry connects established science to the daily realities of communicating with children.

About the author

David A. Smith's four-decade exploration of human patterns began long before he sold his successful business to raise his daughters. From Midwest farm beginnings through entrepreneurship and into single parenthood, he's maintained an insatiable need to understand the "why" behind everything—from how things work to where ideas originate.

Smith's studies span from ancient texts to behavioral science. *The Recognition Series* distills observations from single parenting, entrepreneurship, and extensive interdisciplinary study into practical insights about the invisible patterns that influence us all.

He currently lives in the United States, still asking "why?"

For more information about the Recognition Series,
visit www.recognitionpress.com